LIONS, AND TIGE

From worshipping piles of rock, man advanced slowly, with stops along the way, to enjoy the wildlife. Animal cults are perhaps one of the oldest religious gestures known.

Lions. The lion was associated with the Egyptian gods Re and Horus; there was a lion-god at Baalbek and a lion-headed goddess, Sekhet. The Arabs had a lion-god, Yaghuth. In modern Africa we find a lion idol among the Balonda.

Tigers. The tiger is associated with Siva and Durga, but its cult is confined to the wilder tribes. In Nepal the tiger festival is known as Bagh Jatra, and the worshippers dance disguised as tigers. Tiger-gods are also found in Hanoi and Manchuria.

Bears. Bears were big in Siberia: As recently as 1900, among the Ainu of Sakhalin, a young bear was caught at the end of winter and fed for some nine months. Then after receiving honors it was killed, and the people, who had previously demonstrated grief at its approaching fate, danced merrily and feasted on its body. The bear is traditionally associated with Bern in Switzerland, and in 1832 a statue of Artio, a bear goddess, was dug up there.

THE POCKET PROFESSOR

RELIGION

THE POCKET PROFESSOR

EVERYTHING YOU NEED TO KNOW ABOUT

RELIGION

BY GREGG STEBBEN

SERIES EDITOR: DENIS BOYLES

POCKET BOOKS
New York   London   Toronto   Sydney   Tokyo   Singapore

An *Original* Publication of POCKET BOOKS

POCKET BOOKS, a division of Simon & Schuster Inc.
1230 Avenue of the Americas, New York, NY 10020

ISBN: 0-671-53489-0

First Pocket Books trade paperback printing July 1999

10   9   8   7   6   5   4   3   2   1

POCKET and colophon are registered trademarks of
Simon & Schuster Inc.

Book design by Helene Wald Berinsky
Cover design by Tom McKeveny

Printed in the U.S.A.

RRDH/✖

*This series is dedicated to
Professors Eliot Coleman, Norman Fyster,
Catherine Gira and Stephen Wiest.*

—D.B.

CONTENTS

RELIGION

You know, you start talking about life, and you start talking on a grand scale: lifetime supply. Life-size. Big as life. No, *larger* than life.

It's all hype. Life is a teeny-weeny thing, a passing thought, a divine whim. Life is one of those phases that you eventually outgrow.

Then what? Well, then you find out the truth about religion, that's what. Religion is humankind's most elaborate and ornate creation, an edifice at once terrifying, mythic, consoling, amusing, edifying, and, of course, inspiring. Religion towers above all of human history, a beacon that has led nations to fight wars and create civilizations, make monumental works of art and literature and deeply moving pieces of music, develop intricate legal and ethical systems, and give sanctity to life. Religion has invested our puzzling existence with individual worth and meaning.

Not bad, considering the entire enterprise is built on a foundation of high hope, great fear, and extravagant rumors. So let's be practical autodidacts here. All we want to know is this:

WHAT HAPPENS AFTER YOU DIE?

Just one damned thing after another? A big, white light at the end of a tunnel? A vision of Great-Grandma in fuzzy slippers and a housecoat? Maybe all of those things, maybe more, maybe not. But you'd think that after all the people who have already died, some of them famous and some of them people we have known quite well, we'd have some fixed notion about what *exactly* happened to them. We hope of course that whatever it is, it is something *nice,* something that makes sense of dying and hence adds a little sense to living. But apparently with death, as with its neighbors, war and love, anything goes.

So what does happen after you die? Well, it depends on two things, one having nothing to do with religion and the other having everything to do with religion. First, what happens after you die depends on *what* you were. This is a matter of mere circumstance—geographic, maybe, or ethnic. Second, what happens after you die depends on *how* you were. Here is where we encounter fear and trembling.

Since in matters of faith, everybody knows they're right, all we know for sure about what we believe is that no matter *what* we believe, we're probably at least partially wrong. Netherworld's a big place, you're a long time dead, God's bigger than all creation, and all that.

> All talk about God staggers under impossible difficulties. Yet monotheists have all been very positive about language at the same time they have denied its capacity to express the transcendent reality. The God of Jews, Christians and Muslims is a God who—in some sense—speaks. His word is crucial in all three faiths. The word of God has shaped the history of our culture.
>
> —Karen Armstrong
> *A History of God* (1994)

THE FIVE WORST HELLS

In descending order, of course, they are Zoroastrian, Tibetan, Hindi, Judeo-Christian, and Islamic. Be good or be there.

CONSUMER'S GUIDE TO HEAVENS AND HELLS

WHO DIES	WHAT HAPPENS NEXT—Best-Case Scenario	WHAT HAPPENS NEXT—Worst-Case Scenario
Egyptians	The rich get richer, the poor get poorer. Egyptians believed in a continuation of one's earthly condition in one's earthly body after death, hence their preoccupation with embalming and then placing the body in as well-equipped a tomb as the deceased could afford. The spirits of royalty went on to enjoy a sumptuous eternity, while more common folk frequented their tombs from time to time to enjoy that which was left for them by their relatives. The cult of Re rewarded the aristocrats of the Old Kingdom (c. 2500 B.C.E.) with a solar afterlife. The cult of Osiris, which grew rapidly during the Middle Kingdom (c. 1900 B.C.E.), promised resurrection and eternal life to all, regardless of social status—that is, if the deceased passed the tribunal held at the day of judgment.	Didn't really have a hell. Egyptians loved death and spent their lives and fortunes preparing for it. It was heaven for embalmers, hell for heirs. Sir James George Fraser's *Golden Bough: A Study in Magic and Religion* (12 volumes and an aftermath) is the best source of information on the development of religion and myth, and his volume devoted to Adonis and Osiris is especially useful in comparing Greek, Egyptian, and other religions. Also interesting: Rosalie David's *The Cult of the Sun: Myth and Magic in Ancient Egypt.* A primary source is *The Egyptian Book of the Dead* (edited by Thomas George Allen). **A different sort of afterlife:** In the nineteenth century, Egyptian mummies were used to stoke the fires in Egyptian steam locomotives. There was also a market in export mummies, since, according to an article by Dirk Stratton in the January–February 1992 issue of *Aldus* magazine, paper manufacturers could strip the wrappings off them to make brown paper. Alas, the rags caused an outbreak of cholera.

WHO DIES	WHAT HAPPENS NEXT— Best-Case Scenario	WHAT HAPPENS NEXT— Worst-Case Scenario
Hittites, Phoenicians	Beyond death lay . . . nothing. Still, funerary vaults were furnished and some Phoenicians poured drinking water down a clay pipe into the vault just in case.	Hittite myths speak of a netherworld. We don't know if the dead actually reside there, but one haunting aspect of Hittite beliefs was that the spirit of a dead person with a gripe against a living person might torment the latter until the grievance was resolved. Once the spirit was pacified, it was sent on the road to the abode of the dead.
Sumerians	Not much going on in Sumerian heaven, unless you were a god. A few optimistic Sumerians believed the dead spent eternity in a dreary, poorly lit, depressing shadow world—realm of Nergal, god of the dead, where presumably, they wished they were dead. Or deader.	Sumerians saw the human condition as one of total subordination to the gods. But even the gods reserved a deathless, happy life for themselves, imposing on humankind a precarious spiritual existence. Sumerians, Phoenicians, and, for that matter, Hittites and Babylonians (see following) all were part of a greater Mesopotamian culture. For an introduction, see Robert Watson's *The First Cradle* or Seton Lloyd's *Foundations in the Dust: A Story of Mesopotamian Exploration.* Several important texts survive, including *The Epic of Kumarbi* and Hammurabi's famous legal code. *The Epic of Gilgamesh* (c. 1750 B.C.E.) is an account of a search for immortal life and is the principal source for Sumerian cosmology. It also contains

WHO DIES	WHAT HAPPENS NEXT— Best-Case Scenario	WHAT HAPPENS NEXT— Worst-Case Scenario
Sumerians (cont.)		the first reference to the great flood of later Noah and the Ark fame.
Babylonians	One early Babylonian legend holds there are 14 doors to the underworld; a later one indicates seven doors. Either version seemed to make the Babylonians unhappy enough to consider this life the only one where they had a chance at happiness, however remote or brief—hence, lots of nice gardens in Babylon.	Although Babylonians believed there was no retribution for sinners, there was no hope for saints, either. If you were lucky enough to have been buried at all, you went to dusty, cold, dark prison where, huddled together with other dead folk, you lived out a miserable existence in eternity. If you weren't buried, you were destined to roam the earth and feed on refuse with other unsettled ghosts forever. Babylonian myth is sort of the singles bar of religious study, since it's packed full of demons, man-eaters, and gruesome creatures that are half human, half beast (like Washington, D.C.). See Thomas Winklow's *By the Rivers: An Exploration of Ancient Babylonian Myth and Legend.*
Zoroastrians	Dead Zoroastrians contemplated the virtue of their lives for three days, after which they were judged and led across the Chivat Bridge, the bridge of judgment. *Good* Zoroastrians were met by a beautiful woman, who	*Bad* Zoroastrians were also led across the Chivat Bridge, but they were met by an old crone who escorted them to hell. Given the importance they place on symmetry, it is not surprising that hell for a Zoroastrian is the dark opposite of heaven. In this hell,

WHO DIES	WHAT HAPPENS NEXT— Best-Case Scenario	WHAT HAPPENS NEXT— Worst-Case Scenario
Zoroastrians (cont.)	led them to heaven, a light, airy, and enormously cheerful place, probably full of fruit—sort of like a permanent hospital room. **Thus spake Zoroaster:** No other early religion is so full of influences for Judaism, Christianity, and Islam than Zoroastrianism, a religion that has suffered an extraordinary amount of persecution for the last millennium or so. First articulated by Zarathustra (or Zoroaster), the earliest (c. 7th century B.C.E.) of the great prophets of monotheism, Zoroastrianism emerged from the spirit worship of the Neolithic tribes that settled Persia and India sometime in the second or third millennium B.C.E. Zoroaster himself is an obscure figure, but apparently he was a priest of some sort, married and with children. He experienced a series of visions when he was in his early thirties and began preaching his new religion. His effort to pare down to one the dozens of minor deities that cluttered Neolithic pantheons resulted in violent rejection, but after a decade or so, Zoroastrianism gained a foothold in northern Persia, and then it grew quickly. For the next millennium, Zoroastrianism was one of the world's great religions, with empires of believers stretch-	the emphasis is on rehabilitation, and the punishments in hell often mirror the offenses in life, Dante style. Heaven or hell, dead Zoroastrians had to wait around for yet another final judgment, one that would come only with the arrival of a universal savior. Zoroastrians believe the world is essentially good but threatened by evil. They view the ongoing drama of history as a battle between the good deity and the goodness of humans against the evil deity and his cohorts—death, decay, filth, and bad behavior. Moral and physical purity are important duties of good Zoroastrians. (In fact, so anxious are Zoroastrians to avoid polluting the Earth that their dead are not buried but instead are taken to "sun temples," where they are exposed to the elements and to carrion birds who eat the flesh of the dead. (A peculiar example of such a place is to be found on Zanzibar.) The final judgment will be preceded by the arrival of the true prophet, a man born of a virgin. **Apt quote:** "God sends meat, and the Devil sends cooks." —John Taylor (1580–1653) John R. Hinnells, in *Zoroastrianism and the Parsis* and in

WHO DIES	WHAT HAPPENS NEXT—Best-Case Scenario	WHAT HAPPENS NEXT—Worst-Case Scenario
Zoroastrians (cont.)	ing from Turkey to Pakistan. Cyrus, who liberated the Jews from exile in Babylon, was a Zoroastrian, as were the rulers of Persia who came after him. Zoroastrian priests, called the Magi, were everywhere, including apparently, at the birth of Christ (and for good reason—see below). Persecution of the Zoroastrians began as early as 330 B.C.E. with Alexander the Great. **What every good Zoroastrian believes:** ■ Ethical behavior is linked to salvation, thus establishing in Zoroastrianism the cosmic bribe that gives muscle to most modern religions. ■ All men and women, regardless of social status, exercise free will, and their choices will be the means by which they are judged in the next world. ■ God—called Ahura Mazda—loves humankind, but he is thwarted by the Lucifer of Zoroastrianism, Angra Mainyu, Ahura Mazda's evil twin. The universe is where these two divinities do battle. ■ God created humankind to help him in his battle against Angra Mainyu. He also created a heavenly hierarchy comprising divine beings, rather like archangels.	*Spanning East and West,* provides a good introduction both to Zoroastrianism and to its spinoff cult, Mithraism, one of the most popular religions in the Roman Empire, at least from the second to the fifth centuries. Zoroaster, according to legend, was murdered at age 77 while praying.

WHO DIES	WHAT HAPPENS NEXT— Best-Case Scenario	WHAT HAPPENS NEXT— Worst-Case Scenario
Zoroastrians (cont.)	■ Devout believers anticipate the final conflict between good and evil—a biblical-style apocalypse featuring earthquakes and fires—when the dead will be raised and judged again. The wicked will go to hell. The world will be restored to the perfect state it enjoyed at creation. The righteous will go to heaven. This view of the end of the world and the consequent universal resurrection and judgment had great impact on Judeo-Christian and Islamic concepts of what a happy final judgment ought to be like. Thus, Zoroastrianism was the first religion to offer theories of final judgment, of resurrection, and of free will. The easier belief system offered by Islam—along with 1,000 years of merciless persecution—has almost done in Zoroastrianism. Today, there are just slightly more than 100,000 Zoroastrians left in India, mostly in the precincts of Bombay, and another 15,000 or so in Iran. *Iran.* Yow!	
Jews	Heavenwise, immortality is in the hands of faith and good gossip—at least until the Messiah comes to	Early Hebrew thought placed the dead in Sheol, a place like the one Sumerians went to— dusty and dark—where Yah-

WHO DIES	WHAT HAPPENS NEXT— Best-Case Scenario	WHAT HAPPENS NEXT— Worst-Case Scenario
Jews (cont.)	redeem men's souls and send them to Olam Ha-Ba (literally, "the next world"), a place that forbids eating, drinking, procreation, business, jealousy, hate, and competition. Instead, the "righteous sit with crowns on their heads deriving pleasure from the radiance" of God. Pious Gentiles may be found there, too, provided they have followed the following seven laws: 1. Honor the laws. 2. Abjure idolatry. 3. Abjure blasphemy. 4. Abjure homicide. 5. Abjure sexual promiscuity. 6. Abjure thievery. 7. Refuse to eat the limbs of a living animal. Judaism is the *only* faith with a nondiscriminatory heavenly admissions policy—although faithful Muslims have a better chance of getting in than Christians, whose Trinitarian beliefs may be a problem.	weh promptly forgot about them. Gehenna was a place where some stayed for eternity and some just stopped by for a year before upgrading to heaven. The whole idea was most likely influenced by Zoroastrian ideas of punishment.
Confucianists	Heaven, Confucius say, is a state of positive grace in harmony with the ethical and humanistic spirit of *li*, the essence of propriety and restraint, and in perfect balance of yin and yang. **Yin–yang:** This is the theory of Chinese opposites. Yin is	Confucian hell was not a well-defined place, but the implication of an absolutely hellish existence may be found in an earthly existence bereft of balance and goodness. Confucius (551–479 B.C.E.) was primarily a teacher, not a

WHO DIES	WHAT HAPPENS NEXT— Best-Case Scenario	WHAT HAPPENS NEXT— Worst-Case Scenario
Confucianists (cont.)	the female force, associated with the moon and the Earth. It is dark, passive, and cold. Yang is the masculine force, associated with the heavens and the sun. It is light, warm, and active. According to Confucian thought, the natural order of creation can be explained by the fluctuations and cycles of those two forces.	philosopher; hence, his instructions are heavily influenced by other spiritual disciplines and traditions. But his successful linking of ethical behavior and moral precepts with virtually every aspect of Chinese life—including government—was remarkable. His sayings are collected in the *Lun Yü*.
Taoists	The *Tao*, pronounced with a D, is the cosmic, passive essence of existence. Immortality may be found by becoming part of it. How to get there from here? Various Taoist sects prescribe various methods: Some favor meditation, some prefer ritual and liturgy, some advocate alchemy. In a pinch, exorcism, dieting, and flagellation are also available. But the basic idea is to approach heaven in a state of existence that has no will, no desire, no motive, no nothing.	There are plenty of opportunities for divine punishment in Taoism, ranging from hot and dry places to cold and wet places. It is a religion that has almost as many gods concerned with retribution for bad behavior as there are ways to behave badly. For a thorough if somewhat arid survey, see Herrlee Glessner Creel's *Chinese Thought, from Confucius to Mao Tsê-Tung*.
Hindus	Early Hindu legend said the dead went to heaven and listened to flute songs under a tree with Yama, who was the first man to die, and was also god of death. Later, heaven expanded its pleasures: families were reunited and there was plenty of good sex there.	The truly evil await rebirth in the infernal regions where Yama sits in judgment. Hindus believe in karma, that the body was merely a garment for the soul. Since one lives over and over again, one simply keeps changing clothes. So death is birth, and birth is death.

WHO DIES	WHAT HAPPENS NEXT— Best-Case Scenario	WHAT HAPPENS NEXT— Worst-Case Scenario
Hindus (cont.)	Later, the idea of reincarnation grew in popularity. After dying, you return to Earth to a position in the food chain that more or less reflects your virtue (or lack thereof) in your previous life. As heavens evolved, they also multiplied, each god having one—so they are more or less infinite. Likewise with hells. Jainism, a related faith, is also concerned with the *moksha,* or release from this mortal coil. But Jainism is far more ascetic and far more concerned with the effects of karma. There are perhaps four million Jains, and almost all of them are in India. For more, see Padmanabh S. Jaini's *The Jaina Path of Purification.* Principal Jainist teachings are those of Mahavira, an ascetic of the sixth century B.C.E. who died of starvation on purpose. The movement split in two many centuries ago; the fight seems to be over whether a good Jainist should wear clothes or go naked.	Ancient Hindus held that either extinction or relegation to the realm of darkness beneath the Earth was the fate of those who didn't achieve a heavenly state because they neglected ritual participation. An appropriate image of Hindi hell is one of sitting in torrents of blood chewing on one's hair. Hindis are sect fiends. Hundreds of cults exist, each devoted to the worship of one or more Hindi gods, and each representing a unique degree of sophistication or simplicity. The aim of all Hindis is the same, however—to escape from bad karma and end the ceaseless repetition of deaths and rebirths. Mircea Eliade's *Patanjali and Yoga* is a good introduction to the physical approach to Hindu discipline. At one time, in the late 1960s, virtually every college-age young person in the United States was a Hindu believer of one sort or another, and they were steadfast—until many years later, that is, when they discovered mortgages and sports utility vehicles.
Buddhists	The Buddhist heaven is derived from that of Hinduism and is hierarchical.	Buddhists have eight major hells. There are 16 minor hells to go with each major

WHO DIES	WHAT HAPPENS NEXT— Best-Case Scenario	WHAT HAPPENS NEXT— Worst-Case Scenario
Buddhists (cont.)	There are three major divisions: six heavens of sensual enjoyment, between 13 and 18 heavens of forms, and four heavens of formlessness. But the aim of the game is to attain nothingness, so formlessness is the A ticket. Siddhartha Gautama, the original sixth-century B.C.E. Buddha, saw the desolate nonsense of life and theorized that either there is something better than this or, best of all, *nothing,* which he thought even better still. Hence, reincarnation is the complex path, through life after meaningless life, to nirvana, a state of blissful nothingness, a cosmic void, the shortcut to which is careful meditation and good deeds. Once nirvana has been achieved, you get off the merry-go-round of reincarnation and are at one with the world soul.	hell, for a total hell count of 136. Duration of passage through any one of these hells is not definitely established. It depends on the amount of evil karma to be burned up. In Buddhist hell, adulterers climb thorny trees. Chinese Buddhism was considerably more complex, with lots more heavens, lots more hells, and a complete celestial bureaucracy, with departments run by gods: the Ministry of Thunder, the Ministry of Healing, the Ministry of Fire, the Ministry of Epidemics, and the Ministry of the Five Sacred Mountains, run by the Great Divine Ruler of the Eastern Peak. Edward Conze wrote some helpful introductory texts, including *A Short History of Buddhism* (a Zen book title if ever there was one).
Tibetans	Tibetan religious customs originally had two separate traditions—a regional variation of Buddhism and an older religion called Bon, an import from Persia with a vague touch of Zoroastrianism. The two are now quite similar. Living Tibetans liked the idea of going to the paradise whence Buddha came.	Dead Tibetans usually became nasty spirits and needed conciliation or appeasing. They needed priests to point the way to hell, where they might be punished and then sent along to the Judge of the Dead. Not surprisingly, Tibetans invented some cold hells to

WHO DIES	WHAT HAPPENS NEXT— Best-Case Scenario	WHAT HAPPENS NEXT— Worst-Case Scenario
Tibetans (cont.)		add to the hot ones of Buddhists who didn't live in such a rigorous climate. Eight cold hells they have, the fourth so cold your tongue is paralyzed—and the only thing you can say is *ha ha*. Some joke. Tibetan religious belief is fertile ground for ersatz theological esoterica, in which the illuminati of one group or another are in touch with dead Tibetan monks and the like. For a reasonable survey, see Giuseppe Tucci, *The Religions of Tibet*. The principal sacred text is *The Tibetan Book of the Dead* (translated by Francesca Fremantle and Chögyam Trungpa). The Dalai Lama is the nominal leader of the Tibetan Buddhists, and he has written several books, all of which the prospective autodidact may wish to consult.
Greeks	Early Greeks had no concept of a heaven. There was only a hell. Later Greek beliefs held up the possibility for an afterlife spent in the ritzy neighborhood of the immortal gods, but only for those who had lived a morally upright and ritualistically correct life. By the fifth century B.C.E., belief in an eternal life up among the stars was widespread.	A descent into gloomy Hades was the final stop for the souls of all men, according to early Greeks. Situated where night meets day or in subterranean regions, Hades was a dark, musty world, odious to mortals and immortals. In this country without sunshine or laughter, where all people were obliged to make their way sooner or later, the dead, their heads filled with

WHO DIES	WHAT HAPPENS NEXT— Best-Case Scenario	WHAT HAPPENS NEXT— Worst-Case Scenario
Greeks (cont.)		darkness, wandered forever among silent fields of daffodils, making atonement in the depths for their sins. Thomas Bulfinch's *Age of Fable; or, Beauties of Mythology* provides an anecdotal outline of Greek myth. Fraser's *Golden Bough* (see above, under "Egyptians") or G. S. Kirk's *The Nature of Greek Myths* both provide something better: a useful context.
Romans	Anything could happen to dead Romans, so diverse were their theologies. They might live forever, like good Greeks, next to the gods, or they might return as family spirits, or they might be reincarnated . . .	. . . or they might turn to dust. Franz Valery Cumont's *Astrology and Religion Among the Greeks and Romans* provides a necessary explanation of Roman adaptation of Greek religious structure. An even better, if somewhat harder to find, introduction is Hélène A. Guerber's *The Myths of Greece and Rome*. Michael Grant's *Roman Myths* allows for ground-level entry to this subject. For a contemporary discussion, see Marcus Tullius Cicero's essay, *De natura deorum* (*On the Nature of the Gods*).
Celts	Good, dead Irish traveled across the sea to Tir na n-Og, the land of eternal youth, where the sun was never hidden behind the clouds, and where all the Irish women	Bad Irish stayed in Ireland— no eternal youth for them.

WHO DIES	WHAT HAPPENS NEXT— Best-Case Scenario	WHAT HAPPENS NEXT— Worst-Case Scenario
Celts (cont.)	were beautiful. The major-domo of the place was Lug, an Irish version of Odin. Lug's festival marks the beginning of harvest. Lug was one of the group of Celtic gods driven into the burial mounds by the arrival of Christian missionaries.	
Christians	There's a lot of administrative complexity here, so the Christian heaven may well be a bureaucratic hell. For most species of Christians, death triggers a *provisional* judgment on the fate of the soul. Those condemned go straight to hell. Those judged worthy are saved. If the saved soul belongs to a Catholic, it is purified by a stint in purgatory. Orthodox Christians suffer no distinctly purgatorial delay, but their transit upstairs or down is a slow one. Protestants go to heaven nonstop. But everybody's on probation, since the final fate of all souls is deferred until the Second Coming, when everyone is sent to a final resting place, good or bad.	The Christians borrowed the idea of hell from the Jews and their burning landfill, Gehenna. But, as more than one autodidact has noted, hell is where the Christian imagination has really soared. Arthur Schopenhauer said we are better at imagining hell than heaven because we can draw on more experience. **Apt quote:** "I don't think there's a heaven—but there's certainly a hell. Everything we've experienced on earth seems to point towards the permanence of pain." —Anthony Burgess F. F. Bruce's *New Testament History* may be as good a place to start as any. The main stuff can be found in the Bible.
Incas	Heaven for Incas was a déjà vu–all-over-again kind of thing, insofar as their here-*after* very much resembled	Kidney hell: Incas believed in the existence of a lower world, a cold place where the only food was stones.

WHO DIES	WHAT HAPPENS NEXT— Best-Case Scenario	WHAT HAPPENS NEXT— Worst-Case Scenario
Incas (cont.)	their *here,* but the food was much better.	The Mesoamerican religions of the Incas, the Mayans, the Aztecs, and others are introduced in Friedrich Katz's *Ancient American Civilizations.*
Moslems	According to the Koran, "Paradise is better than anything in the world. . . . Around [the believers] shall go eternal youths with goblets, ewers, and a cup of flowing wine. No headache shall they feel therefrom, nor shall their wits be dimmed. They shall be served by large-eyed damsels of modest glance." But get this: There are *72* damsels per believer in Mussalman heaven, and traditional interpretation speculates that the male believer will have more vigor wooing these large-eyed damsels than he had on earth, by a factor of about 100 to 1. Just kidding. Don't shoot!	The damned are broiled until the skin is extra crispy, then given a new skin. The fire is 70 times hotter than on earth. There are no loopholes; new skins are provided for eternity. Plus, individuals are made bigger so they suffer more. Later Moslem thought indicates nasty business for sinners. They are roughed up by two angels, then smooshed into the ground and bitten by serpents with huge mouths. There are three principal divisions in Islam. The Sunnites are the most populous and are conservative believers in determinism. The Shiites, made famous recently by ayatollahs and kidnappers, are more emotional believers in free will and the infallibility of the 12 *imams,* or great teachers, whose wisdom will lead the Shiites to heaven. The Sufis are Islam's mystic wing, believers in the revealed inner vision of Allah. The *hilal,* the Islamic crescent, has been viewed as a sort of Moslem version of the cross since the Crusades. Moslems

WHO DIES	WHAT HAPPENS NEXT— Best-Case Scenario	WHAT HAPPENS NEXT— Worst-Case Scenario
Moslems (cont.)		didn't see it that way, though, until the late eighteenth century. Now, usually with a star, it's the predominant symbol of Islam. Sir Hamilton Gibb's *Islam: A Historical Survey* is an excellent introduction to the subject.

A QUICK BACKGROUNDER ON GOD

There are some awkward questions we eventually have to ask about God. One good question is whether He was miraculously discovered or simply invented. Traditional religious thought holds for the former; God is a revealed truth. Skeptics claim people invented God. To the faithful, this is an alarming view, since it obviously clears the way for God to be uninvented, should He provoke too much trouble. Ultimately, this argument can have no satisfactory conclusion; doubters cling to external truths. Believers suggest that God simply reveals Himself as He pleases.

EGYPTIANS

The earliest written records indicate that religion was already well established in prehistory. Egyptian theology, among the earliest studied, developed around the three main gods in the Egyptian pantheon: Re or Ra, the sun god, and all that stands for; Set, who evolved into a god of evil; and Osiris, the most important historically. He died and then rose from death, an act the pharaohs tried to emulate by perfecting the art of embalming.

MESOPOTAMIANS

The Mesopotamian idea of supreme beings was more formal than that of the Egyptian. The Mesopotamian world—essentially, the Tigris and Euphrates River valleys—was divided into four parts,

---

SEVEN NATIVE AMERICAN CREATION MODELS

■ **Diving Bird** or other creature plunges to the bottom of the primordial sea and emerges with mud, which is shaped into a universe by a coyote or other cunning critter

- **Cosmic sex,** in which the earth-mother couples with the sky-father
- **Metamorphosis** of creation, from primeval nothing to developed something
- **Theft** of fire or water or other basic building-block by a fox, coyote, or other "trickster"
- **Web spinner** who weaves the spidery net of creation
- **Spare parts** from the body of a fallen monster or giant become us: Parts "Я" Us
- **Teamwork,** in which a father and son, twin brothers or dual heroes work together to make a creation they can call home

---

THE SOPHISTICATION OF GOD

The argument about the evolution of God is continued not only by such pop theologians as William Irwin Thompson but also by such mainstream religious thinkers as Hans Küng in his book *Does God Exist? An Answer for Today.*

---

each with its own deity whose importance was measured by how well his soldiers performed in battle and how much land they conquered. A successful god, a god figure—like that of the Hittites, for example—gave his people many rewards, but immortality wasn't among them. This made for many unhappy Mesopotamians. The tale of Gilgamesh illustrates the quest for immortality and the failure to achieve it.

These early cultures profoundly affected the direction in which the idea of God in the West would go, but the religion that most influenced early Western religious concepts was the cult of Yahweh. Yahweh was apparently an early desert god, descended, perhaps, from nothing more than a mound of stones in the corner of a field and worshipped to ensure the fertility of the field. The slow evolution of this deity mirrored, more or less, the political successes of his worshippers. Finally, his followers believed, Yahweh made a specific covenant at a specific time to lead his people to victory—provided they forswore all other gods save him.

The monotheistic tradition that evolved from this cult still influences most of the concepts around which Western peoples view their spiritual world.

Harry Elmer Barnes, in *An Intellectual and Cultural History of the Western World,* parallels the evolution of our modern God with the development of increasingly sophisticated political structures.

POODLE WORSHIP

It hasn't been a straight track, though. From worshipping piles of rocks, humankind advanced slowly with stops along the way to enjoy the wildlife. Animal cults are perhaps one of the oldest religious traditions known. Here, according to the late great Northcote Whitbridge Thomas, is the hairy pantheon as it existed at the beginning of the twentieth century:

ANIMAL PANTHEON	
CRITTERS	**PERSONAS AND PRACTICES**
Bears	Bears were popular in Siberia: As recently as 1900, among the Ainu of Sakhalin, a young bear was caught at the end of winter and fed for some nine months; then after receiving honors, it was killed, and the people, who had previously demonstrated grief at its approaching fate, danced merrily and feasted on its body. Among the Gilyaks, a similar festival was found, but there it took the form of a celebration in honor of a recently dead kinsman to whom the spirit of the bear was sent. There is a good deal of evidence to connect the Greek goddess Artemis with a cult of the bear; girls danced as "bears" in her honor and could not marry before undergoing this ceremony. The bear is traditionally associated with Bern, Switzerland. In 1832 a statue of Artio, a bear goddess, was dug up there.
Buffaloes	The Todas of southern India abstained from the flesh of their domestic animal, the buffalo. Still, once a year they sacrificed a bull calf, which was gobbled up in the forest by the adult males. Native Americans also had a spiritual relationship with the buffalo, since the animal provided for many of their basic needs.
Cattle	Cattle are objects of obsession by many pastoral peoples; they live on milk or game, and the killing of an ox is a sacrificial function. Conspicuous among Egyptian animal cults was the cult of the bull Apis, whose birthday was celebrated once a year. Pure white oxen would be sacrificed to Apis. Women were forbidden to approach the animal. After its death, it was mummified and buried in a rock tomb. Less widespread was the cult of the Mnevis, also consecrated to Osiris. Similar observances are still found on the upper Nile; the Nuba and Nuer worship the bull; the Angoni of central Africa and the Sakalava of Madagascar keep sacred bulls. In India, respect for the cow is widespread but is of post-Vedic origin; there is little actual worship, but the products of the cow are important in magic.

CRITTERS	PERSONAS AND PRACTICES
Crows	The crow is the chief deity of the Thlinkit Indians of the North American Arctic. All over that region, it is the chief figure in a group of myths, fulfilling the office of a culture hero who brings the light and gives fire to humankind. Together with the eagle hawk, the crow also plays a great part in the mythology of southeastern Australia.
Dogs	Actual dog worship was uncommon until quite recently. The Nosarii of western Asia were said to worship a dog. The Kalangs of Java had a cult of the red dog, each family keeping one in the house. According to one authority, the dogs are images of wood that are worshipped after the death of a member of the family and burned after 1,000 days. In Nepal, dogs are worshipped at the festival called Khicha Puja. Among the Harranians, dogs were sacred, revered as brothers.
Elephants	In Siam—now Thailand—it is believed that a white elephant may contain the soul of a dead person, perhaps a Buddha. At one time, when such an elephant was captured, its captor was rewarded and the animal was brought to the king to be kept ever afterward. It would never be bought or sold. It was baptized and feted and mourned for like a human being at its death. In some parts of Indochina, the belief is that the soul of the elephant may injure people after death; it was therefore feted by the whole village. In Cambodia, it is held to bring luck to the kingdom; in Sumatra, the elephant is regarded as a tutelary spirit. The cult of the white elephant is also found at Ennarea, southern Ethiopia, and at garage sales everywhere.
Fish	Dagon, the merman god of fertility worshipped by the Philistines and throughout the ancient Middle East, seems to be a fish god with human head and fish body. Worshippers wore fish skins. In the temples of Apollo and Aphrodite were sacred fish, which may point to a fish cult. Atargatis is said to have had sacred fish at Askelon, and from Xenophon we read that the fish of the Chalus were regarded as gods.
Goats	Dionysus was believed to take the form of a goat, probably as a divinity of vegetation. Pan, Silenus, the satyrs, and the fauns were either capriform or had some part of their bodies shaped

CRITTERS	PERSONAS AND PRACTICES
Goats (cont.)	like that of a goat. In northern Europe, the wood spirit Ljesche was believed to have a goat's horns, ears, and legs. In Africa, the Bijagós are said to have a goat as their principal divinity.
Hares	The Algonquin tribes had as their chief deity a "mighty great hare" to whom they went at death. According to one account, the hare lived in the east; according to another, in the north. In his anthropomorphized form, he was known as Menabosho or Michabo.
Hawks	In northern Borneo, there appears to be an evolution of a god in the three stages of the cult of the hawk among the Kenyahs, the Kayans, and the sea Dayaks. The Kenyahs will not kill it, they continually thank it for assistance, and formerly, they consulted it before leaving home on an expedition; it seems, however, to be regarded mostly as a messenger of the supreme god Balli Penyalong. The Kayans have a hawk god, Laki Neho, but seem to regard the hawk as the servant of the chief god, Laki Tenangan. Singalang Burong, the hawk god of the Dayaks, is completely anthropomorphized. He is the god of omens and ruler of all the omen birds, but the hawk is not his messenger, for he never leaves his house. Stories are told, however, of his attending feasts in human form and flying away in hawk form when all was over.
Horses	There is some reason to believe that Poseidon, like other water gods, was originally conceived in the form of a horse. In the cave of Phigalia, Demeter was, according to popular tradition, represented with the head and mane of a horse, possibly a relic of the time when a nonspecialized corn spirit bore this form. Her priests were called colts. In Gaul, we find the horse goddess Epona; there are also traces of a horse god, Rudiobus. The Gond in India worship a horse god, Koda Pen, in the form of a shapeless stone, but it is not clear that the horse is regarded as divine. The horse or mare is a common form of the corn spirit in ancient Europe.
Leopards	The cult of the leopard is widely found in West Africa. Among the Ewe, a man who kills one is likely to be put to death; no leopard skin may be exposed to view, but a stuffed leopard is worshipped. On the Gold Coast—now Ghana—a leopard hunter who has killed his victim is carried around the town behind the

CRITTERS	PERSONAS AND PRACTICES
Leopards (cont.)	body of a leopard; he may not speak and he must besmear himself so as to look like a leopard and imitate its movements. In Loango, a prince's cap is put on the head of a dead leopard and dances are held in its honor.
Lions	The lion was associated with the Egyptian gods Re and Horus; there was a lion god at Baalbek and the lion-headed goddess Sekhet. The Arabs had a lion god, Yaghuth. In modern Africa, we find a lion idol among the Balonda.
Lizards	The cult of the lizard is most prominent in the Pacific islands, where it appears as an incarnation of Tangaroa. On Easter Island, a form of the house god is the lizard; it is also a tutelary deity in Madagascar.
Mantises	Cagn is a prominent figure in Bushman mythology; the mantis and the caterpillar, Ngo, are his incarnations. The mantis was called the "Hottentots' god" by early settlers.
Monkeys	In India, the monkey god Hanuman is a prominent figure. In pious villages, monkeys are safe from harm. Monkeys are said to be worshipped in Togo. At Porto-Novo, in the region once called French West Africa, twins have tutelary spirits in the shapes of small monkeys.
Serpents	The cult of the serpent is found in many parts of the Old World. It is also not unknown in the United States. In Australia, on the other hand, though many species of serpents are found, there does not appear to be any species of cults.
	In Africa, the chief center of serpent worship was the former Kingdom of Dahomey, but the cult of the python seems to have been of exotic origin, dating back to the first quarter of the seventeenth century. By the conquest of Whydah, the Dahomeyans were brought into contact with a people of serpent worshippers and ended by adopting from them the cult that they at first despised. At Whydah, the chief center of the former Kingdom of Dahomey (now Benin), there is a serpent temple, tenanted by some 50 snakes. Every python must be treated with respect, and death is the penalty for killing one, even by accident. The ser-

CRITTERS	PERSONAS AND PRACTICES
Serpents (cont.)	pent god has numerous wives, who, until 1857, took part in a public procession from which the profane crowd was excluded; a python was carried around the town in a hammock, perhaps as a ceremony for the expulsion of evils. The rainbow god of the Ewe was also conceived to have the form of a snake. His messenger was said to be a small variety of boa, but only certain individuals, not the whole species, were sacred. In many parts of Africa, the serpent is looked on as the incarnation of deceased relatives; among the Amazulu, as among the Betsileo of Madagascar, certain species are assigned as the abode of certain classes; the Masai, on the other hand, regard each species as the habitat of a particular family of the tribe.

In the United States, some of the Amerindian tribes reverence the rattlesnake as grandfather and king of snakes who is able to provide fair winds or cause a tempest. Among the Hopi of Arizona, the serpent figures largely in one of the dances. The rattlesnake was worshipped in the Natchez temple of the sun; and the Aztec deity Quetzalcoatl was a serpent god. The tribes of Peru are said to have adopted great snakes in the pre-Inca days; and in Chile the Araucanians had a serpent figure in their deluge myth.

Over a large part of India, there are carved representations of cobras (*nagas*) or stones as substitutes. To these, human food and flowers are offered, and lights are burned before the shrines. Among the Dravidians, any cobra that is accidentally killed is burned like a human being; no one would kill one intentionally. The serpent god's image is carried in an annual procession by a celibate priestess.

Serpent cults were well known in ancient Europe. We learn from Herodotus of the great serpent that defended the citadel of Athens; the Roman *genius loci* took the form of a serpent. A snake was kept and fed with milk in the temple of Potrimpos, an old Slavonic god. To this day, there are numerous traces in popular belief, especially in Germany, of respect for the snake, which seems to be a survival of ancestor worship; the "house snake," as it is called, cares for the cows and the children, its appearance is an omen of death, and the life of a pair of house snakes is often held to be bound up with that of the master and mistress themselves. Tradition says that one of the Gnostic sects known as the Ophites caused a tame serpent to coil around the sacramental bread and worshipped it as the representative of the Savior.

CRITTERS	PERSONAS AND PRACTICES
Sheep	Only in Africa do we find a sheep god proper. Ammon was the god of Thebes. He was represented as ramheaded and his worshippers held the ram to be sacred; however, a ram was sacrificed once a year, and its fleece formed the clothing of the idol.
Tigers	The tiger is associated with Siva and Durga, but its cult is confined to the tribes; in Nepal, the tiger festival is known as Bagh Jatra, and the worshippers dance disguised as tigers. The Waralis worship Waghia, the lord of tigers, in the form of a shapeless stone. In Hanoi and Manchuria, tiger gods are also found.
Wolves	Both Zeus and Apollo were associated with the wolf by the Greeks, but it is not clear that this implies a cult of the wolf. The wolf is frequently found among the tutelary deities of North American dancing or secret societies. The Thlinkits had a god, Khanukh, whose name means "wolf." They worshipped a wolfheaded image.

WHO YA GONNA CALL?

God travels under assumed names. Do not be distraught or confused: You'll know Him when you see Him. Alas, many do not see Him until they need Him.

THE NAMES OF GOD

Religious/Ethnic Group	Deity Names
Zoroastrianism	Ahura Mazda
Judaism	Yahweh; Jehovah
Buddhism	None; Buddha
Egyptians	Ammon; Re
Sumerians	Anu; Enlil; Ea
Babylonians	Marduk
Assyrians	Ashur
Greeks	Zeus
Romans	Jupiter
Hinduism	Ishvara (as a conceptual supreme deity); other principal gods: Brahma (the World-Soul), Vishnu, and Shiva Nataraja
Maoris	Io

Islam	Allah
Hittites	Teteshhawi (more of an "eternal essence" than a god, but as close as Hittites come)
Bantu	Iruva, Leza, Nzambi, Mulungu (regional variants)
Fon (West Africa)	Mawu and Lisa (male and female creation deities)
Mayans	Quetzalcoatl

The historical development of the Western concept of God is also the province of historical theology, a field plowed thoroughly by the well-known Anglican theologian William Oddie of Oxford. His most recent book is *What Will Happen to God? Feminism and the Reconstruction of Christian Belief.* Sir James George Fraser's *Golden Bough* gives a more dimensional picture of the evolution of the abstract nature of God. Ditto Harry Elmer Barnes's *An Intellectual and Cultural History of the Western World.*

THE BASIC ELEMENTS OF RELIGION

These disparate beliefs also share other common threads. According to most theologians, here's what's needed to make a real religion. Without these, you're chanting in the dark:

- Divine revelation
- Prophecy
- Priests (or other officers)
- Sacrifice
- Sacraments
- Pilgrimage
- Self-denial
- Meditation
- Mysticism

THE ELEMENTS OF A CULT

Cults, meanwhile, exist as a sort of parody of religious belief. Make a cult successful enough, and you have a religion. Until then, it's still a cult, and as we've sadly seen, cults can kill.

- The leader is a charismatic who demands total allegiance.
- The cult's doctrine mandates a suspension of rational debate.
- A cult uses unscrupulous recruitment techniques.
- A cult creates a dependency on the part of the believer.
- A cult manipulates a member's fears and feelings.
- A cult has an overriding interest in its own survival to the exclusion of all else.
- A cult uses members as a cheap or free labor pool.
- A cult insists on isolation from the outside world.
- A cult will seek to break apart family units.
- A cult is based on a worst-fear scenario.
- A cult is Machiavellian.
- The cult's financial arrangements and status are kept secret from the members and from outsiders.
- There is often implied violence on some level of a cult's activities.

Before you hand over that large inheritance, read the *Encyclopedic Handbook of Cults in America,* by J. Gordon Melton.

MAIMONIDES' THIRTEEN ARTICLES OF FAITH

To see how the elements of religion combine—sometimes subtly, sometimes noisily—to inform a faith, read Moses Maimonides's articles. They give an idea not only of the beliefs of most Jews at the end of the Middle Ages, but they also provide a starting point for understanding the nature of modern Western religious beliefs:

1. The existence of God
2. The unity of God
3. The incorporeality of God
4. The eternity of God
5. The obligation to worship God alone
6. Prophecy
7. The superiority of the prophecy of Moses
8. The Torah as God's revelation to Moses
9. The immutability of the Torah

10. God's omniscience
11. Reward and punishment
12. The coming of the Messiah
13. The resurrection of the dead

Maimonides (1135–1204), a Spanish-born physician, was one of the great Jewish theologians, not only codifying rabbinical law and ritual (in *Mishneh Torah*), but also providing a working synthesis of Aristotelian and Jewish thought (in the *Guide for the Perplexed*).

DEFERRED PAYMENT PLANS

The deferment of the payoff may well be the telling factor in a religion's success. Look at the evidence:

- With *Zoroastrianism,* you die but then have to wait until the end of time to be redeemed. There are almost no Zoroastrians left.
- With *Judaism,* you die but then have to wait until the Messiah appears to lead His people before resurrection. Evangelical Judaism hasn't met with much success lately. Converts to Judaism are so rare, relatively speaking, that the most famous convert of late is perhaps Sammy Davis Jr.
- With *Christianity,* you get a quasi save, but for the upgrade to full eternity, you have to wait until the Second Coming and the Final Judgment, also called the Rapture by some Christians with an apocalyptic sense of poetry. Fundamental Christianity, with its emphasis on heaven tomorrow, has been doing well, but, surprisingly, so have orthodox doctrines, like Roman Catholicism and Eastern Orthodoxy.
- *Islam* is coming on strong, principally because of its user-friendliness and its immediate payback for good behavior. With Islam, you're saved immediately, no red tape, no probation.
- Small wonder, then, that *secular religions,* with their shrinks and cults and gyms and seminars and tapes and self-absorption, are doing best of all, since with these you don't have to wait until you die to make good. *You can have it all now!* At least for a while.

Anyway, this what-happens-next issue has yet to be decided. But it should be noted here that underlying all these beliefs is a central concern, namely that death does not alter humankind's enduring, if occasionally tense and often misunderstood, relationship with God.

It should be noted that as we can see from the table of heaven and hells on pages 3 through 17, in answering the question "What happens after you die?" all major religions participate in the great cosmic bribe, a variation on "If you're very good, you can stay up past bedtime and watch TV." If this is less than satisfying, then it should also be noted that providing the answer to what happens after life is interesting only from humankind's point of view. From God's point of view, perhaps the purpose of life is not for us to survive death but to give us the opportunity to come to know God through faith—no matter what happens after we die.

GOOD BOOKS

Most major faiths come with a technical manual containing all the instructions you need to build a better life on Earth and an immortal life in the hereafter. Common threads: divine inspiration (or, in the case of Islam, divine authorship), an intertwined concept of ethics and religious responsibility, and an exaltation of life.

NEXTOLOGY

The concept of final judgments, last days, immortality and the hereafter is addressed by eschatology (from the Greek *eschatos*, last, or furthest, and *logos*, science), a theological discipline that has fallen into obscurity especially since the secularization of Western religious traditions. This is an odd development, really, given first that the implications of death are everywhere throughout our lives and second that eschatology (at least on the personal scale) lives in the what's-in-it-for-me neighborhood of theology and hence is very contemporary indeed. But modern theology, now marketed—absurdly—as something "relevant," has simplified things

THE BIBLE

The Bible, one of the most influential books in history, is a Judeo-Christian coproduction, in which the Hebrew holy book—the Old Testament—provides the basis for the Christian sequel—the New Testament.

THE TORAH

The Torah (or Pentateuch) comprises the five books of Moses (Genesis, Exodus, Leviticus, Numbers, and Deuteronomy) and is seen as evidence of the

Covenant. (See page 26 for Maimonides' Thirteen Articles of Faith.) The rest of the Old Testament is divided into the Prophets (Joshua, Jeremiah, and the rest) and the Writings (which includes Job, the Psalms, the Song of Solomon, and others).

THE TALMUD

The Talmud, which contains articles of Jewish law and commentaries on the law, is divided into two sections: the Mishnah, which offers simple statements of the law, and the Gemarah, which offers the commentaries. The Mishna contains 4,000 articles divided into six areas of concern: agriculture, rituals and holy days, marriage, civil laws, sacrifices, and holy men. The authoritative Babylonian Talmud was compiled circa 550.

Orthodox Jews believe in an absolute interpretation of the Torah and the binding nature of its laws, whereas Reformed Jews accept only its ethical guidance. In between these two positions are Conservatives and others. An introduction may be found in Isaac Epstein's *Judaism.*

considerably: You die, then you go to heaven, which, we get the feeling, is somewhat bland and politically correct, but otherwise quite a nice place. No doubt there are quotas in heaven, all part of affirmative salvation. Americans are very fond of heaven, and most modern American theologians will argue that everybody gets saved and goes to heaven, since it's only fair.

Aspirational eschatologists should read Lars Nilsen Dahle's *Life After Death and the Future of the Kingdom of God* and the appropriate chapters in Frank Byron Jevons's *An Introduction to the History of Religion.*

WHAT MAKES THE GOOD BOOKS GOOD		
RELIGIOUS TEXT	READERS	BEST PARTS
The Avesta	Zoroastrians	The Avesta contains the 17 hymns, called the Gathas, that contain Zarathustra's teachings.
The "Confucian canon"	Confucianists	Contains five "classics" and four "books." **The classics:** ▪ The *Sho Ching,* a collection of ancient speeches and documents

RELIGIOUS TEXT	READERS	BEST PARTS
The "Confucian canon" (cont.)	Confucianists	■ The *Shih Ching,* an assortment of several hundred ancient poems and songs ■ The *I Ching,* the famous book on divination based on the principles of yin and yang ■ The *Ch'un Ch'iu,* a local history of Confucius' home state, Lu ■ The *Li Ching,* an anthology of ancient rituals **The books:** ■ Confucius' own sayings ■ A collection of Mencius' teachings on ethics (*Meng-tzu*) ■ The *Chung Yung,* or The Doctrine of the Mean ■ The *Ta Hsüeh,* or The Great Learning
Tao-te Ching	Taoists	The *Tao-te Ching,* supposedly written by Lao-tzu in the fourth century B.C.E., is contained in the Taoist canon of sacred books—the *Tao Tsang,* which was assembled much later. The *Tao Tsang* contains three "vaults" and four "supplements," each concerned with various aspects of ritual, philosophy, meditation, and spirits. The best-selling book of Oriental spirituality, the *I Ching,* is actually a Confucian teaching text of Chinese Buddhism (see below), although much influenced by Taoist thought.
Holy texts	Hindus	The *Veda,* which contains the *Upanishads,* the *Ramayana,* and especially the *Bhagavad-Gita.* For a

RELIGIOUS TEXT	READERS	BEST PARTS
Holy texts (cont.)	Hindus	gloss, try R. C. Zaehner's *Hinduism* (as well as his *Hindu Scriptures*).
The Tipitaka	Buddhists	The *Tipitaka* is the sacred text containing Siddhartha's teachings. Other commentaries are contained in various *sutras*. The *Kama Sutra*, for instance, points the way both to good sex and to Tantric Buddhism, a highly ritualized form of Buddhism that involves magic, esoteric philosophy, and some good swiving beneath a blue lightbulb. Zen Buddhism involves helpful disciplines to meditative clarity, whereas the ancient line of teachings leading to Mahayana Buddhism stresses purity of thought and awareness of existence.
The Koran	Moslems	The Koran, of course, is the sacred text of Islam. Organized into 114 *suras,* or chapters, believers maintain it contains the words of Allah. The Prophet's sayings are collected in the *Hadith*. **The Five Pillars of Islam:** The Koran places the responsibility for a correct religious life on the believer. God grants certain privileges to the believer who fulfills God's demands. These duties are the Five Pillars of the faith: 1. *Confession of faith*—Usually translated as "There is no God but Allah, and Muhammad is His prophet." 2. *The ritual of prayer,* which is performed five times daily—at daybreak, noon, midafternoon, after sunset, and in the early

RELIGIOUS TEXT	READERS	BEST PARTS
The Koran (cont.)	Moslems	part of the night. The ritual is a series of movements and recitations called a bowing and resembling an Orthodox Christian prostration. Different numbers of bowings are prescribed for different times. They are made facing Mecca, ideally with others and in a mosque. 3. *The giving of alms* 4. *Fasting during the day during the month of Ramadan.* Since the lunar year is shorter than the solar year, this is a movable fast, going through all seasons in about 33 years. 5. *At least one pilgrimage to the sacred mosque at Mecca,* health and wealth permitting. The pilgrimage itself consists of a series of further rituals. **The rules of *jihad:*** Here are the rules for holy war, Moslem style, according to the *Shariá* (Islamic law): ■ *Before they are vanquished, unbelievers must first be invited to embrace Islam.* If they "follow a sacred book"—as, for example, do Christians and Jews—and are not idol worshippers, they are given a three-way choice among becoming Moslems, submitting to Islamic rule under a treaty of protection and tribute, or fighting it out. ■ *If they accept Islam, their lives, families, and property are secure,* and they form henceforth part of the Moslem community. The ability of Islam to create a com-

RELIGIOUS TEXT	READERS	BEST PARTS
The Koran (cont.)	Moslems	mon feeling between highly different races is one of its most striking features. ■ *If they surrender, they pay a poll tax, their personal safety is ensured, and they are given a distinctly inferior status,* having no technical citizenship in the state but only the status of protected "clients" (*dhimmi*s). ■ *If they elect to fight, the door of repentance is open, even when the armies are face to face.* But after defeat, their lives are forfeit and their families are liable to slavery and all their goods, to seizure. It is up to the Islamic conqueror whether to put them to death, to enslave them, to give them their liberty, or to exchange them for Moslem prisoners. ■ *As for their families and wealth, these may be released only with consent of the army that has captured them.* ■ *Apostates must be put to death.* ■ *Four fifths of the booty after a battle goes to the conquering army.* Got a problem with that?

BAD BOOKS

No, no, not really *bad*—just not quite good enough. The term *apocryphal* doesn't necessarily mean "false" so much as it means "not accepted as true." There is a large stack of apocryphal writings roughly contemporary with the Old and New Testaments that, although often possessing valuable historical insights and some pretty good stories, have nonetheless been dismissed as not bearing the divine stamp of approval. Many of the New Testament–era documents are Gnostic (cult) propaganda or otherwise heretical. Some are simply not particularly revelatory. Among the most interesting:

JUDEO-CHRISTIAN APOCRYPHA DIGEST

BOOK	CONTENTS
The Book of Jubilees	Written in Hebrew by a Pharisee in the heyday of the Maccabeans. He looked for the immediate advent of the messianic kingdom, which was to be ruled by a messiah provided by the reigning Maccabean family. The kingdom would involve the gradual transformation of nature and the ethical transformation of humankind.
Life of Adam and Eve	There are a bunch of apocryphal books starring Adam, Eve, the snake, the apple, the leaf, the whole ugly mess. Among the other titles in the series: Death of Adam, Creation and Transgression of Adam, Expulsion of Adam from Paradise, Penitence of Adam and Eve, and Conflict of Adam and Eve with Satan. Some of these were written by Christians.
Pirke Aboth	In rabbinical lit, this book is held in esteem equal to that given the book of Proverbs. The book is a collection of sayings attributed to some 60 Jewish teachers. Most of it was compiled in the years C.E. 70 to 170, but some is from much earlier.
Gospel According to the Egyptians	In this one, dating from the first century C.E. or so, Christ is going to return to undo the work of women. The distinctions of sex are to come to an end, and consequently, there'll be no need for marriage. The book is a nasty piece of pantheistic Gnosticism.
The Book of James	Mary lives as a perpetual virgin in the temple, while the brothers of Jesus turn out to be sons of Joseph by a previous marriage. Written circa C.E. 110.

BOOK	CONTENTS
Gospel of Judas Iscariot	Lousy turncoat Judas Iscariot spills beans, confesses all, begs for mercy. Today, he'd be a victim of loyalty deficit disorder.
Gospel of Mary	A Gnostic report on the progress of the soul through the seven planets. There are other Gospels of Mary, by the way. Most of them are Gnostic documents.
Acts of Paul and Thecla	This, the earliest of Christian romances (probably before C.E. 150), recounts the adventures and sufferings of a virgin, Thecla of Iconium. Based on a true story, as they say in Hollywood. In most Acts of Paul documents, Nero sentences Paul to death.
Acts of Peter	Peter battles Simon Magus, a famous magician who toyed with Christianity one too many times. In this document, Nero sentences Peter to death.
Acts of Thomas	A Gnostic tract dating from the early second century C.E. Like the Gospel of Thomas, it is somewhat rambling and diffuse, but basically carries the Gnostic message that Christ not only was the Son of God but was also the first mystic.
Teaching of the Twelve Apostles	A discussion of ethical instruction and church rules and discipline. Along with the Apostolic Constitutions, another apocryphal document, it is used by Orthodox Christians in the *Pedalion.*

A POCKET HISTORY OF THE JEWS

SCAPEGOATS

Judaism, more than any other religion in history—save perhaps only Zoroastrianism—has been defined as much by its persecution as by its practice.

> A common feature of ghetto and *shtetl* life was the quest for *yichus,* an untranslatable word most closely akin to "prestige" and "status." Possessing *yichus* was much like charm in a woman—if she has it, it makes no difference what else she has.
>
> —Max I. Dimont
> *Jews, God, and History* (1962)

Although Judaism was a relatively small regional religion until the conquest of Palestine by the Romans in the first century B.C.E., by the end of the second century C.E. there was a substantial Jewish community dispersed throughout Europe. Prejudice against Jews wasn't unusual before the birth of Christ, but anti-Semitism became a well-refined art under the early Christian church, and by the end of the third century C.E., anti-Semitism had become an institutionalized aspect of Christian spiritual hegemony in Europe. Early Christians saw the Jews in the stereotypical anti-Semitic terms that still exist today. To them, Jews were Christ killers. They bore the collective burden of deicide or they were guilty of the desecration of the sacrament or they were guilty of murdering Christian children to use their blood to make Passover loaves or they were guilty of failing to see the Messiah when He finally showed up or they were guilty of all of the above. Or, to eliminate complexity, they were devils. An inquisition against the Jews was launched in the fifteenth century, and by the end of the medieval period, Jews had been made scapegoats for political failure everywhere. Forbidden to own property, excluded from virtually every segment of commercial life save money lending and some crafts, Jews were forced out of nearly every country in Europe at one time or another and were subjected to vicious pogroms, including systematic rape, pillage, and murder.

This blood lust against the Jews has continued apace throughout the course of modern European history and finally culminated in the second world war's Holocaust, the attempted genocide of the Jews by Germans. Anti-Semitism survives today in Poland, Russia, and other places where there are barely enough Jews left alive to carry the blame placed on them.

JEWISH DEVILS

For all those anti-Semites who just can't get it right, here's a spotter's guide:

DEVILISH NOMENCLATURE	
Dybbuk	A *dybbuk,* from Jewish folklore, is an evil soul or spirit of a wicked dead person who has entered a live person, speaks through the person's throat and causes much discomfort and spiritual distress—tonsils from hell. *Between Two Worlds, or The Dybbuk,* an early silent film based on the famous Yiddish drama by Shloime Ansky, is one of the most overlooked movies of all time, bar none. It's on videotape. Paddy Chayefsky's *The Tenth Man* also involves a *dybbuk.* There are several *dybbuks* in ancient literature: ■ Mastemah (Enmity), in the Book of Jubilees ■ Belial, in the Testaments of the Twelve Patriarchs ■ Angel of Darkness, in the Dead Sea Scrolls

---

The prolonged harassment and dispersal of the Jews had two completely different but equally important effects: First, assimilation became imperative. For many Jews, the important theological concepts of heaven, hell, redemption, revelation, and the rest were overwhelmed by similar Christian concepts, so that by the mid-twentieth century, for example, many U.S. Jewish children were never offered instruction in the nature of a Jewish heaven or a Jewish hell. Instead, they were taught the importance of the law and the significance of tradition and left to discover for themselves other critical aspects of Judaism—but often only in the context of a highly attractive, somewhat ethically lackadaisical Christian culture.

The excesses of Western culture have succeeded where history failed. Today, there are far more secular, nonobservant Jews than there are observant Jews.

Two useful additions to your reading list are Jacob Katz's *Exclusiveness and Tolerance: Jewish–Gentile Relations in Medieval and Modern Times* and Paul Johnson's highly readable *History of the Jews.*

The second effect of Judaism's history of persecution, one that altered forever worldwide Jewry, was the division of Judaism into two distinct groups, the Ashkenazim and the Sephardim.

THE ASHKENAZIM AND THE SEPHARDIM

The rise of Islam during the seventh, eighth, and ninth centuries and the deterioration of political structures in Europe during the Middle Ages resulted in a neat split between the Christian countries of the West and the Moslem countries of the East.

The Jews living in the West—and especially in central and eastern Europe—came to be called Ashkenazim, from *ashkenazi,* which means "Germanic." Separated from the rest of Jewry, the Ashkenazim developed their own language—Yiddish, based on medieval German—their own customs, their own music, literature, drama, and their own interpretation of the Talmud. Today, the Ashkenazim dominate Jewish intellectual and creative life, and constitute the larger of the two groups.

The Sephardim are the descendants of the Jews who were expelled from the Iberian Peninsula (Sepharad means "Spain") at the end of the fifteenth century and who settled in the Near East, northern Africa, and, to a lesser extent, in northern Europe. Their dominance of the Jewish communities in the Middle East has resulted in the heightened political influence of the Sephardim in Israel. The customs and traditions of the Sephardim reflect, to a measurable extent, the Islamic culture that for centuries has surrounded them.

The distinctions between the two groups are such that today in Israel, each supports its own chief rabbi.

These aren't the only groups of Jews separated by history. The Falasha Jews in Ethiopia, for example, have little in common with either the Ashkenazim or the Sephardim. By and large, Islamic nations treated Jews much more fairly than did the Christian nations of Europe. For an examination of the differences and similarities of these two

> I am one member of one people confronting these closing decades of the twentieth century. Whether it knows it or not, my people is now engaged in an attempt to create for itself a third civilization. I feel myself part of that venture. I think of Sumer and its rushing rivers, Egypt and its rising Nile, Canaan and its terraced hills and fertility cults, Greece and Rome, Islam and Christianity, Jerusalem, Babylon, Cordova, Toledo, the Rhine Valley, the Ukraine, Vilna, Odessa, Kishinev. What will Jewry make of itself for the next thousand years?
>
> —Chaim Potok
> *Wanderings: Chaim Potok's History of the Jews* (1978)

> In New York City, more Jews go to a shrink than go to a temple.
> —Stand-up comic Richard Elbin

groups, see H. J. Zimmels's *Ashkenazim and Sephardim: Their Relations.* For a completely fascinating and compelling account of the relationship between Coptic Christians and Falasha Jews in Ethiopia (and for a grand adventure story about the search for the lost Ark of the Covenant), see Graham Hancock's *Sign and the Seal: The Quest for the Lost Ark of the Covenant.*

ORTHODOX, REFORM, AND CONSERVATIVE JUDAISM

In addition to the geographical and historical divisions that have altered Judaism, three distinct theological traditions have also emerged largely in response to varying Talmudic interpretations and social pressures: Orthodox, Reform, and Conservative.

THREE BRANCHES OF JUDAISM	
THEOLOGICAL TRADITION	**HISTORY AND BELIEFS**
Orthodox	Orthodox Judaism, as a distinct tradition, developed in the early nineteenth century and regards itself as the only true Judaism.
	▪ Orthodoxy demands a complete belief in *halakah,* which is rabbinic jurisprudence over Jewish faith both in interpersonal and ritual performance.
	▪ Orthodoxy is synonymous with the classical rabbinical teachings and the authoritative words of the Torah.
	▪ Every aspect of Orthodox life demands strict adherence to the commandments, dietary laws, Sabbath observance, daily prayer, and traditional Jewish liturgy.
	▪ Orthodox Jews have a high regard for the rabbi as teacher and interpreter of the law and place heavy emphasis on education and traditional teachings.
	▪ Most Orthodox Jews believe adjustments to the modern world can be made as long as they do not conflict with the teachings of the Torah.
	Modern problems have also had an impact on Orthodox belief:
	▪ Recognition of the nation of Israel and participation in the World Zionist Organization
	▪ Cooperation with all Jews in matters of secular concerns

THEOLOGICAL TRADITION	HISTORY AND BELIEFS
Orthodox (cont.)	■ A flexible perception of *halakah* ■ Participation in such aspects of general culture as the arts, university life, and the sciences
Reform	Reform Judaism had its beginnings in Germany in the late eighteenth century, partly in response to Enlightenment ideals and partly in response to the changes that had overtaken traditional Jewish society. Rejecting the teachings of the Torah as factual and binding and seeking to make changes in ritual law and worship, the movement was initially based on the theories of Moses Mendelssohn, but it quickly divided into moderate and radical wings. Moderates wanted simply to update those aspects of Judaism based on tradition, not law. The radicals saw a wholesale revision of Judaism, essentially stripping it down to its ethic and monotheistic roots. Generally, radical reformers gained the ascendancy in the United States, whereas the moderates retained influence in Europe. Reform practice includes: ■ The abandonment of dietary laws ■ The introduction of prayers spoken in the vernacular rather than Hebrew ■ Coeducational worship ■ In some congregations, Sunday worship, rather than observing the Sabbath on Saturday
Conservative	In 1850, Jewish leaders, such as the eminent scholar Zacharias Frankel, found themselves unable to identify with Orthodox doctrine and disenchanted with the widespread changes wrought by the Reform movement. Frankel felt Orthodoxy rejected scientific investigation of Judaism, whereas its approach in matters like *halakah* was extremely rigid. The Reform movement, Frankel noted, took a radical approach to religion but failed to distinguish between ritual precepts.

THEOLOGICAL TRADITION	HISTORY AND BELIEFS
Conservative (cont.)	Moreover, he felt the reformers had largely abandoned Hebrew and rejected every aspect of Jewish nationalism and ethnicity. Frankel advocated a middle approach in which the Jewish people and Jewish traditions would be central to Judaism and Jewish law and in which *halakah* would be observed but modified to the needs of the day.
	▪ Critical investigation of the Torah is accepted and used.
	▪ The intellectual basis is a scholarly, historical understanding of Judaism as a structure capable of absorbing modern knowledge without radically changing classic philosophy.
	▪ The Conservative movement takes an holistic approach, seeking to maintain and preserve rituals and ethics laws, practices, and beliefs with universalism and nationalism.
	▪ Its commitment to the *halakah* process and the importance of ritual distinguishes Conservative Judaism from Reform thought.
	▪ It also differs in its flexible and evolving nature, its pluralism, and its acceptance of open theological and scientific inquiry.
	▪ It sees Judaism as an amalgam of religious and ethnic nationhood that has evolved from biblical times.
	In the United States, Conservative Judaism is the largest of the three branches.

For a quick survey, see *The Encyclopedia of Judaism,* edited by Geoffrey Wigoder. For an autodidactic approach, consult C. M. Pilkington's *Teach Yourself Judaism,* which reads very much like a standard catechism.

THE HASIDIM

There have been a number of other splits in the ranks of Judaism, of course, most notably, the Reconstructionist movement of the 1920s. But no other Jewish movement has caused a stir quite like that caused by the Hasidim.

Hasidism was founded in Poland in 1730 by Israel Baal Shem Tov, called the Besht, a charismatic widely known as a miracle worker of sorts and an illumined Cabalist (see The Cabala, page 44). The movement promoted a passionate devotion to God expressed in singing, dancing, and ecstatic prayer and, in keeping with its mystical priorities, declared that personal service to God was more important than the observance of the Jewish laws. The movement flourished by giving hope, interest, and excitement to people who were frightened, deprived, and disillusioned by worship through study.

Outwardly, Hasidic life seemed dour, but it contained within a joyful spirituality. The movement played down the asceticism of conventional rabbinical religious practice: Hasidic leaders were more spiritual gurus than scholars, acting as intermediaries between followers and God.

Poland and the Ukraine were especially receptive to Hasidism, but the movement met strong opposition from established Jewish leaders and communities; Hasidic followers were threatened with excommunication and even betrayed by other Jews to mostly hostile state authorities.

There is no Hasidic orthodoxy; various leaders have created many different branches of Hasidism. Shneur Zalman, for example, the influential Hasidic philosopher, brought his brand of Hasidic practice into common acceptance in the early nineteenth century.

Modern Hasidism resemble Orthodox believers in most respects, although they still follow the movement's characteristic alternative to traditional rabbinical orientation.

For more information, see Harry M. Rabinowicz's *The World of Hasidism.*

THE TRIBES OF ISRAEL

Hasidism, Orthodox, Ashkenazim—none of these schismatic splinters of Jewry have anything on the original 12 tribes of Israel, the shattering of Abraham's descendants into a quarreling clutch of sometimes competing, sometimes warring clans. According to the Bible, the 12 tribes are the troubled descendants of Jacob's 12 sons, born of two of Jacob's wives, Leah and Rachel, and of their maidservants. There were

- Leah's six sons, Reuben, Simeon, Levi, Judah, Issachar, and Zebulun
- The sons of Bilhah (Leah's maidservant), Dan and Naphtali
- Rachel's sons, Joseph and Benjamin
- The sons of Zilpah (Rachel's maidservant), Gad and Asher

The boys begat, and their children begat, and so on, until they formed tribes. Then the tribes divided into clans and then subdivided into families, and pretty soon, they were fighting like cats—and not only among themselves, but also with the Canaanites, whose land they took. The kingdom of the Israelites grew until about 1000 B.C.E.: a "golden age"—lasting perhaps only a century or so—of Hebrew victories under Saul, David, and Solomon ended with the death of Solomon in 925 B.C.E., at which time the kingdom split in two. Judah held Jerusalem, and the arid plain to the south, Israel—home to 10 of the original tribes—occupied an area that today would include northern Israel, Lebanon, and part of Syria. (The smallest tribe, the Benjaminites, sort of played the middle.) Eventually, the northern kingdom fell prey to a series of vicious Assyrian attackers, and in 722 B.C.E., Israel was brutally vanquished by the Assyrians under Sargon II. Cities were leveled, entire populations murdered, and, according to Sargon's *Annals of Khorsabad*, nearly 30,000 Israelites were taken away to Assyria and Chaldeans, Babylonians, and other subject peoples were sent by the Assyrians to settle Israel in their stead. The survivors probably assimilated with their conquerors, but the mythic proportion of the Israeli defeat fueled the myth of the historic 10 lost tribes (see box at right). The biblical

> **THE 10 LOST TRIBES**
>
> After the northerners' defeat by the Assyrians, there was a widespread dispersal of the Israeli tribesmen who survived the conquest. Consequently, "lost" tribes have been popping up ever since, and in the oddest places—Ethiopia, China, Yemen, Saudi Arabia, and even in South America. To this day, the Jewish communities of Kurdish, Indian, and Bukharan origin claim descent from the northern kingdom of Israel, as do the Falasha Jews of Ethiopia and the Manipuri Jews of northeast India. So, for that matter, do the non-Jewish people of the Yoruba tribe in Nigeria. Rastafarians toy with the idea, too, since they see themselves as the true Jews who will be redeemed by the ascension of a messiah, Ras Tafari, to the imperial throne of Ethiopia. How else to explain the existence of those people? For one explanation, see Eugene Gold's *The Extinction of Samaria: Israel 800–650 B.C.E.*

account of the decimation of Israel is found in 2 Kings, especially chapter 17. Judea, by the way, survived until 587 B.C.E., when its people were enslaved and Jerusalem and the temple built by Solomon were destroyed by the victorious Babylonians.

Many scholars doubt the biblical account of the origin of the 12 tribes and suggest that these individual groups were thrown together through the pure circumstance of regional geography. *The Tribal History: Theory on the Origins of the Hebrews,* by William Duffy, presents all sides, but Paul Johnson's *History of the Jews* is an even better and more readable introduction.

THE CABALA

The Cabala (or Kabala, Kaballa, Caballah, Cabbala, and so on) is the common word used to describe Judaic mystical traditions developed in the Middle Ages. Like other mystical disciplines, Judaic mysticism seeks a personal union with God—some kind of direct link with the infinite, an intuited vision of divinity achieved through meditation, spiritual exercise, or contemplation.

Cabalistic tradition teaches that creation resulted from 10 *sefirot,* or emanations, of the Godhead. These emanations maintain the balance that provides humankind with a knowledge of God and imbues it with divine energy. But Cabalist mystics also believe there is a capacity for evil in this emanatory balance, and that this evil capability can be unleashed by mankind's sins.

The cosmology imposed by the Cabala is mirrored in the complex esoteric interpretation of Judaic ritual, in its labyrinthine theology, and in its vigorous mythic images.

The Cabala is one of the central elements of Hasidism (see page 41), along with other legal and philosophical practices and concerns.

The most important work on the Cabala is the *Zohar,* thought to be written and edited by Rabbi Moses de León in thirteenth-century Spain. It is the holy book of Jewish mysticism. Others are the *Sefer Yetsirah* (Book of Creation), written before the sixth century, and *Sefer Hasidim* (Book of the Pious), a compilation of mystical legends and study written in 1217. For a more basic study, see *Jewish Legends,* by David Goldstein.

The origins of Jewish mysticism can be found in the first chapters of Genesis and Ezekiel of the Old Testament.

Alphonse Louis Constant (as "Eliphas Levi") proposed a Cabalistic approach to divining with tarot cards, in which each of the trump cards was used to make connections between the *sefirot*. (See Constant's *History of Magic*.)

HOW TO CONDUCT A SEDER

The focus of the seder—a Hebrew word meaning "order"—is the celebration of the God-guided and divinely ordained exodus from Egypt, a central event in the history of the Jewish people. Because the exodus marks the beginning of Jewish sacred history, it is referred to repeatedly in Jewish liturgy and thought.

The seder marks the first evening of Passover, which begins on the fifteenth day of the month of Nisan and continues for seven days. For more information, see *Jewish Holidays: A Guide and Commentary,* by Michael Strassfeld.

This isn't dinner in front of the TV: A seder is a liturgical celebration, not a holiday dinner party. It has specific guidelines that must be observed. The rituals and symbols (see The Seder Plate, below) in the celebration represent both the bitterness of slavery and the great joy of liberation, and the recitation of the *Haggadah,* the liturgical text that recounts the epic of the exodus, provides the ecclesiastical focus for the event.

The Passover seder is a family holiday because of the great importance it places on telling the story and meaning of Passover to the next generation. Only after every crumb of *hametz,* the leavened bread, has been removed (requiring painstaking hours of searching) can the seder take place. The seder should start as soon as possible after sundown, because children should be awake for the entire seder celebration.

The Seder Plate

Of course, everything prepared for the meal must be kosher and not contain a drop of yeast. The seder plate contains all the symbols of the seder:

- *Karpas:* A green vegetable, symbolizing rebirth and spring. It is dipped in salt water near the start of the seder.
- *Maror:* Bitter herbs, either unadulterated horseradish or romaine lettuce

- *Haroset:* A mixture of apples, nuts, wine, spices. The *maror* is dipped into the *haroset* during the seder.
- *Beitzah:* A roasted, scorched hard-boiled egg, left in its shell
- *Zeroa:* A roasted, scorched shank bone

Also, three matzoth, one on top of another, are covered with a napkin and placed next to the seder plate. There should be enough kosher wine for each person to have four cups, although kosher grape juice may be used for the young or intolerant. Other necessary items are

- Salt water in which to dip the *karpas.*
- Elijah's cup, which is an ornate goblet set aside for the symbolic visit of Elijah to the home.
- A *kittel,* which is a white robe worn by the leader of the seder.
- For reclining, to the left side, pillows with pillowcases—or armchairs—are needed for each participant. For a bird's-eye view of how it looks, see the facing page.

Seder Prep
Don't neglect administrative details:

- Decide if you want the seder to be conducted by a leader or by the group.
- Determine exactly how everyone will be involved. For example, will the *Haggadah* be read by one person, by the group, or in rotation?
- Will it be permissible to ask questions or add comments during any part of the celebration?
- If non-Jews are present, figure out how they will be accommodated.
- Decide to what extent children will be involved.
- Decide what you may want to add or omit from the *Haggadah.*
- Make sure you've provided a copy of the *Haggadah* for each person.

List of Key Words and the Order of the Seder Ritual
- *Kiddush:* The *kiddush,* the sanctification of the day, is recited over the first cup of wine, which participants should drink

PASSOVER (PESACH): THE SEDER MEAL

1. *Haggadah* (Passover ritual book), one for each celebrant and visitor
2. Elijah's Cup, kept for the prophet's return
3. The three matzoth (unleavened bread)
4. Candles for holy day
5. Cups of wine, each celebrant drinks four to recall God's four promises of redemption
6. *Betzah* (roasted egg), a symbol of new life and hope
7. *Karpas* (spring)
8. *Maror* (bitter herbs, usually with 7 and 9 reminders of suffering)
9. Salt water
10. *Haroset* (paste made with apple, nuts, cinnamon, and wine) symbolizes the mortar of ity
11. *Z'roah* (roasted shank bone of lamb) recalls the Passover
12. Seder dish, often ornate with six matching dishes

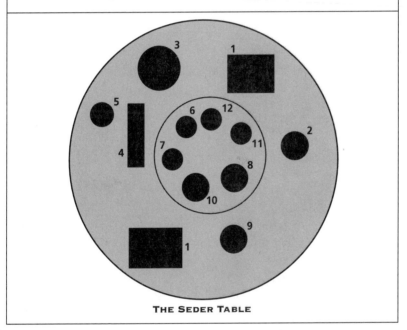

THE SEDER TABLE

while reclining. The *kiddush* ends with the recitation of the *she-he-heyanu* blessing.

- *Urhatz:* Washing of hands.
- *Karpas:* First dip the vegetable in salt water. Then dip the *maror* into the *haroset;* this is done to provoke the children into asking one of the Four Questions, "Why do we dip twice?" The breaking of bread may be done at this point, but the bread is not eaten.

- *Yahatz:* Take the middle of the three matzoth and break it into two. The smaller piece is replaced between the two matzoth, and the larger piece is set aside as the *afikomen,* the matzo eaten at the end of the meal. It is traditional for the children to steal the *afikomen* and hold it for ransom, since the seder cannot end until the *afikomen* is eaten. The seder plate is now removed.
- *Maggid* portion of the seder:

  - *Ha lahma anya:* This is the heart of the *Haggadah,* the story of the exodus. The *ha lahma anya* is recited, an invitation for all who are hungry to join. The invitation ends with an expression of hope for freedom in the land of Israel. The second cup of wine is poured.
  - *Mah Nishtanah:* The Four Questions. This section is usually recited by the youngest child, though anyone can ask, "Why is this night different?"
  - *Avadim hayinu:* Sets forth the two major themes of the *Haggadah,* that all Jews were slaves in Egypt and that the story of the exodus must be told and retold.
  - *Arba-ah vanim:* The Four Questions. Children are told about the exodus.
  - *Mi-tehilah ovdei:* "In the beginning, our ancestors worshiped idols."
  - *Barukh shomeir:* The text that tells of God's redemption and how it will be repeated in every age.
  - *Arami oveid avi:* Deuteronomy 26:5–8 is recited. Ends with recitation of the 10 plagues. It is customary to remove a drop of wine from the cup at the mention of each plague. These are quite difficult to interpret; sometimes a general conversation about the Passover theme may be helpful after the recital.
  - *"Dayeinu":* A song that recalls the great deeds of God performed for the Israelites.
  - *Rabban Gamliel hayah omeir:* An explanation of the central symbols of the seder.
  - *Be-khol dor ve-dor:* Stresses that present-day Jews as well as ancestors are redeemed.
  - *Le-fikhakh:* Includes two sections of the *Hallel.* One part, fur-

ther explaining the exodus, is done now, and the rest of the *Hallel* is recited after the meal.

- The conclusion of the *maggid* section, praising God for being the redeemer: The second cup of wine is drunk, over which participants recite a blessing while reclining.

- *Rahtzah:* Ritual washing of hands. Recite the blessing *al netilat ya-dayim.*
- *Motzi-matzah:* Take the three matzoth and recite two blessings, eating from the top and middle matzoth while reclining.
- *Maror:* Dip the bitter herbs in *haroset* and recite the blessing for *maror.*
- *Korekh:* Take the bottom matzo and make a sandwich with the *maror.* This is the recitation of a temple practice. Eat the sandwich while reclining.
- *Shulhan Orekh:* Eating of the festive meal.
- *Tzafun:* Ransom the *afikomen* from the children and eat it while reclining.
- *Barekh:* The prayer after the meal is recited. The blessing for wine is recited over the third cup of wine, which participants then drink while reclining. This last part of the *Haggadah* ends with song and with praise for the redemption.
- *Hallel:* The rest of *Hallel* is recited. Preceding the *Hallel,* a goblet is placed on the table and a door is opened by a child for Elijah's visit. According to tradition, Elijah will come to herald the Messiah and the final redemption.
- *Shfokh hamatkha,* Psalm 136, and the prayers of *Nishmat* and *Yishtabah:* These are all recited. The blessing over wine is also recited, and participants drink the fourth cup of wine while reclining. Finally, the blessing after wine is recited.
- *Nirtzah:* The conclusion of the seder. A part of the poem *"Hasal Siddur Pesah"* is recited, followed by *le-shanah haba-ah.* A number of songs are sung, including the Song of Songs.

CHRISTIANITY

There are about 1.7 billion Christians on the planet, making it the religion of preference for more people than any other. It's the most successful of many contemporary Middle Eastern messianic cults.

		A GENEALOGY OF
WHO AND HOW MANY	DATE ESTABLISHED	HISTORY
The Orthodox Church: approximately 300 million members	circa C.E. 30 Devout Orthodox recite one of Christianity's oldest prayers, the Jesus Prayer ("Lord, Jesus Christ, Son of God, have mercy on me, a sinner") as a part of the personal mysticism required by Orthodox belief. J. D. Salinger provides a peculiar but not altogether inaccurate view of one of the effects of the Jesus Prayer in *Franny and Zooey.*	The church of the Greek East and the established church of the Byzantine (Eastern Roman) Empire. The Roman Catholic Church was part of the universal church until 1054. Orthodoxy is united by its liturgical theology but divided into its national churches. In the United States, there are competing jurisdictions—a situation forbidden by church canons. Theologically, Orthodoxy is virtually unchanged since the first century. Most liturgical expressions have antecedents going back to the second century. Some of the writings of the Orthodox Church fathers are compiled in the *Philokalia* (4 volumes so far, published by Faber and Faber).

CHRISTIAN DENOMINATIONS

PRINCIPAL BELIEFS AND RITUALS	ETHICAL AND DOCTRINAL STARCH AND ADMINISTRATIVE STYLE	SUPPLEMENTAL OR LITURGICAL BOOKS OR TEXTS
eternal life gained through faith and good works. Venerations of Mary, the *theotókos* ("God Bearer"). Intercession of saints, use of icons as "windows into heaven," primacy of the Trinity. Firm belief in the sanctity of all human life. Seven sacraments: (infant) baptism, marriage, confession and penance, confirmation, communion (Eucharist), ordination, and anointing of the sick. Principal differences between Orthodoxy and Catholicism: Orthodoxy rejects doctrinal additions made unilaterally by the Western church after the first seven Ecumenical Councils, including the doctrine of papal infallibility, the supremacy of Rome, and celibate clergy (although all Orthodox bishops are chosen from among monks and are therefore celibate). Because of a different view of Original Sin, the Orthodox Church also does not require a belief in the Immaculate Con-	Absolute ethical system reinforced with traditional doctrine established at the first seven Ecumenical Councils (held between 325 and 757) at which all the patriarchs of the church were represented. Canons of the church are collected in the *Rudder* (Pedalion). They include forbidding communion to mimes. Orthodoxy has an episcopal hierarchy, with governing patriarchs (the most senior of which is the ecumenical patriarch of Constantinople) and many national churches—Greek, Serbian, Bulgarian, Albanian, even. In most parts of the world, there is a single jurisdictional authority for each country. In the United States and Europe, however, there are many jurisdictions, most of them united in faith and, for the most part, in a common agreement on what constitutes church Tradition. The goal of every Orthodox act of worship is to suggest the majesty and beauty of heaven on Earth, and the goal of every Orthodox Christian is to be a living icon of Christ. When you talk about Orthodox Tradition, the capital *T* matters: Tradition is what Roman	Prayer books galore. The Divine Liturgy of Saint John Chrysostom is the principal eucharistic rite. Western liturgies are also used by some Orthodox, notably those in the Western Rite Vicariate of the Antiochian Orthodox Church. All Orthodox rituals are ancient, ornate, extremely evocative, and cordial to prayer and mysticism. *The Orthodox Church,* by Timothy Ware (Bishop Kallistos), and *A Pocket History of the Orthodox Church,* by Father Aidan Keller, are both useful for providing a survey of Orthodox Christianity.

WHO AND HOW MANY	DATE ESTABLISHED	HISTORY
The Orthodox Church (cont.)		
Roman Catholics: 1 billion	circa C.E. 30 Schism with Orthodoxy in 1054. Eastern Catholic churches recognize the	The church of the Latin West. Legend has Peter as first bishop of Rome (pope). Final split came

PRINCIPAL BELIEFS AND RITUALS	ETHICAL AND DOCTRINAL STARCH AND ADMINISTRATIVE STYLE	SUPPLEMENTAL OR LITURGICAL BOOKS OR TEXTS
eption. The Orthodox Church does, however, condemn abortion and considers artificial birth control to be a matter for confession. In the United States, though, where the larger seminaries are increasingly liberal and where there has been no recent, clear pronouncement on birth control by church hierarchy, many priests routinely permit artificial birth control, simply assuming, incorrectly, that the church has accepted the practice. This is especially true in the Greek Orthodox archdiocese, the most liberal of American Orthodox jurisdictions.	Catholics call the "Deposit of Faith"—the unchangeable doctrines of the church as expressed in canons, apostolic and patristic writing, and long local practice, among other things. Relatively trivial matters of tradition are the source of much internal Orthodox feuding. A more serious divide over the use of the civil (Gregorian) calendar threatens Orthodox unity, since the new calendar was imposed by force and without conciliar agreement. Orthodoxy has a strong, influential contemplative tradition (*hesychasm*). The phenomenal Monastery of Saint Catherine on the Sinai Peninsula and the cluster of monasteries at Mount Áthos are all Orthodox. The Athonite monasteries constitute a semi-autonomous "republic," although Greece handles most civic chores. No women are allowed on Mount Áthos. In fact, no females of any kind—save birds, mice, and cats—are allowed there.	
ternal life gained through faith and good works. Intercession of saints. Veneration of the	Absolute ethical system reinforced with traditional doctrine and the teaching of the hierarchy. Episcopal with papal pri-	Since Vatican II, it's every bishop for himself. In the United States, the

WHO AND HOW MANY	DATE ESTABLISHED	HISTORY
Roman Catholics (cont.)	papal authority of the bishop of Rome, but retain Orthodox liturgical traditions and some aspects of Orthodox theology.	after five centuries of disputes between the eastern and western churches. The last straw for the East: the insertion by Rome, without any ecumenical authority, of *filioque*—the words "and from the Son"—in the Creed, in describing the procession of the Holy Spirit. *Filioque* originated as a Spanish theo-fad, but when Charlemagne seized on the device as a means of taking a swipe at the Byzantines, the Roman church went along.
Baptists: 35 million in many subdivisions and sects (see Variations on a Baptist Hymn, pages 86 to 87)	1609	Radical reformers demanding church–state separation and abolition of infant baptism.
Methodists: 21 million	1738	Anglican breakaway.

PRINCIPAL BELIEFS AND RITUALS	ETHICAL AND DOCTRINAL STARCH AND ADMINISTRATIVE STYLE	SUPPLEMENTAL OR LITURGICAL BOOKS OR TEXTS
Virgin Mother and belief in the Immaculate Conception of Mary. Seven sacraments (see above, under The Orthodox Church). Firm belief in the sanctity of all human life.	macy. Authoritative and legalistic. Belief in papal infallibility of pronouncements made *ex cathedra* (in the pope's capacity as pastor and teacher).	Eucharistic liturgy of the Roman Catholic Church has more in common with Protestant liturgies than with traditional Catholic rites. This does not hold, however, for Eastern Catholics, many of whom use Orthodox liturgies.
Salvation through grace and revelation. Baptism by immersion usually at age 12 (or after the "age of accountability," which is at whatever age a child voluntarily professes belief in Christ and is perceived to truly comprehend that belief), communion (Lord's Supper).	Somewhat absolutist. Doctrinally informal. Congregational.	
Salvation by faith and striving for perfection. Infant baptism, communion (Lord's Supper).	Quite situational of late, but originally quite absolute. Doctrine of methodical Bible study and interpretation formulated by John Wesley. Episcopal in	

WHO AND HOW MANY	DATE ESTABLISHED	HISTORY
Methodists (cont.)		
Lutherans: 38 million	1517	Martin Luther, a song-writing ("A Mighty Fortress Is Our God" and others) priest, protested the sale of indulgences and other Roman Catholic practices by nailing a list of 95 complaints to the church door in Wittenberg, Germany.
Anglicans: 70 million (nominal), including U.S. Episcopalians	1534	Established by Henry VIII to subordinate church claims to state power.
Presbyterians: 28 million	1557–60	Established as a reform church in Scotland by John Knox in 1560 and based on the teachings of John Calvin (1509–1564), a theologian who established a theocracy in Geneva in the mid-sixteenth century.

PRINCIPAL BELIEFS AND RITUALS	ETHICAL AND DOCTRINAL STARCH AND ADMINISTRATIVE STYLE	SUPPLEMENTAL OR LITURGICAL BOOKS OR TEXTS
	administration, congregational in worship.	
Salvation by faith alone, not by works. Infant baptism, communion (Eucharist).	Somewhat situational. The Bible is the final arbiter of doctrine. State religion in northern European kingdoms, where the structure is episcopal. Mostly congregational in the United States.	
Salvation by faith and good work, but, more recently, salvation obtainable by good works. Infant baptism, communion (Eucharist).	Completely situational, once quite absolutist. Episcopal with nominal primacy of the archbishop of Canterbury. Since 1970, deeply divided over such issues as ordination of women and homosexual priests. Since the late 1980s, more than 1 million members (of 2.7 million) lost in the United States alone.	*The Book of Common Prayer and Administration of the Sacraments and Other Rites and Ceremonies of the Church*
Salvation by faith and grace. Some traditional Presbyterians still adhere to a belief in predestination. Infant baptism, communion (Lord's Supper).	Somewhat situational. Doctrine stresses primacy of God in daily life. General synod with representational system for lay and clergy.	

WHO AND HOW MANY	DATE ESTABLISHED	HISTORY
Pentecostals and fundamentalists: 100 million	1900–present	Ongoing reformation of Protestantism, generally with an emphasis on charismatic leaders and the primacy of scripture and revealed truth. Growing very fast in the Third World.
Church of Christ: 2.5 million	1804	Established to protest Protestantism's declining evangelical fervor.
Jehovah's Witnesses: 1.5 million	1896	Established to save souls in the belief in an imminent Second Coming.
Mennonites: 250,000	1572	Swiss reformers eager to reclaim Orthodoxy.
United Church of Christ, Congregational Christian Church, other Protestant groups: 5 million	1720–present	Coalescing movement of liberal, nondoctrinaire Protestant groups.

RINCIPAL BELIEFS ND RITUALS	ETHICAL AND DOCTRINAL STARCH AND ADMINISTRATIVE STYLE	SUPPLEMENTAL OR LITURGICAL BOOKS OR TEXTS
alvation by faith. Rituals an include speaking in ongues, faith healing, xorcism, Bible thump-ng, and other emotional isplays. Baptism of reborn" believers, com-munion (Lord's Supper).	Somewhat absolute. Doctrines are simple and fundamental, with authority placed in the Scriptures. Congregational.	
alvation by faith. Adult aptism, communion ord's Supper).	Absolute. Doctrines are simple and Scripture based.	
alvation by faith and itnessing. These are the Vatchtower people who ome calling when ou're in the shower.	Absolute. Believers in Arianism (see Heresies: A Guide to Unwelcome Ideas, page 102). Rejects government authority and most medical procedures; believes other churches are satanic.	
alvation by faith. Pri-nacy of scripture. Adult aptism, communion ord's Supper).	Absolute. Rejection of modern technology and some govern-ment authority (especially in military and education). Amish Mennonites are the ones that drive the cute buggies in Penn-sylvania.	
alvation by faith. Infant aptism, communion ord's Supper).	Situational. Congregational. Some national organizations.	

WHO AND HOW MANY	DATE ESTABLISHED	HISTORY
Mormons (Church of Jesus Christ of Latter-Day Saints): 3.2 million	1827	Based on visions of Joseph Smith and on the contents of the *Book of Mormon,* a divine revelation. Overcame early persecution to become one of the fastest growing faiths in the world.
Unitarian Universalist Church: 1.2 million	1779	Descended from skeptical Christian and Arian thought.

The two principal elements that bind the religion together are the use of the Bible as the primary sacred text and the belief in resurrection and eternal life through the sacrifice of Jesus Christ. Beyond that, everybody in Christendom's got a different answer.

BROAD CATEGORIES

The spectrum of Christianity in the United States today may be divided into roughly four primary colors. They may overlap, but they each have sometimes subtle but important differences, like politics in Ireland.

INCIPAL BELIEFS ID RITUALS	ETHICAL AND DOCTRINAL STARCH AND ADMINISTRATIVE STYLE	SUPPLEMENTAL OR LITURGICAL BOOKS OR TEXTS
ılvation through faith, ꜭod works, and witness-ꜭg. Adult baptism, com-ꜭunion (Lord's Supper), ꜭcret temple rituals.	Rather absolute. Insistence on temperance and physical purity. Centralized administration.	*The Book of Mormon*
ꜭerybody's saved, pro-ꜭded there's a heaven—ꜭo sure thing in ꜭnitarianism, where, ꜭspite its Christian ori-ꜭns, there is only a ꜭgue and nonbinding ꜭreement that there is a ꜭod at all. Some congre-ꜭtions mimic Christian ꜭtuals.	Extremely situational, with a firm if unfocused reliance on ethical correctness and humani-tarian concerns.	Many or none

■ First, *the liturgical churches,* including the Roman Catholics but especially the Orthodox. Some Anglican churches—especially the Anglo-Catholic traditionalists—also belong in this category. All of these see worship as the central act of organized religious life. Although the liturgies are all different, they have each been derived from the traditions of Christianity over the years of its existence.

The principal Eucharistic liturgy—called the Mass by the Western churches, and the Divine Liturgy by the Eastern church—is divided into two main parts. The first half is

devoted to teaching the word of God; the second, to the celebration of the Eucharist. These liturgies are conducted by an
official with special rights, generally a priest. Until recently,
the Roman Catholics and Episcopalians believed the ongoing
orthodoxy of liturgy and traditions of worship provided an
important avenue for religious experience. The Orthodox still
adhere to this belief. Ironically, the so-called Liturgical movement in the Roman Catholic church in the United States since
Vatican II has profoundly secularized traditional forms of
Catholic worship, removed much of its mystery, and
attempted to impose a rationalization on something as inherently irrational as faith.

With few exceptions—some Old Catholic groups, for example—women are not admitted to the priesthood of these
churches.

Dom Gregory Dix's *Shape of the Liturgy* is the standard work
on the development and history of Christian ritual, but John
Mason Neale—like Dix, an Anglican—also provides a thorough examination of the liturgies of the Eastern churches in
his *Primitive Liturgies.* For an Orthodox view try Fr. Alexander
Schmemann's *Introduction to Liturgical Theology.*

∎ Second, *the Word and sacrament denominations,* chiefly Lutheran
and Presbyterian, the moderate conservatives. They honor tradition, but it is not the standard under which they operate.
Where the liturgical churches see the role of priest-as-celebrant
as central to belief, in Word and sacrament denominations, the
minister is important mostly for preaching the message of the
Bible, not as the official celebrating communion. The Bible, and
not tradition, is the only authority for both faith and action.

∎ Third, *the Protestant liberals, or the experiential denominations—*
the Methodists, Congregationalists, and the more conservative
Baptists. These groups have little interest in ecclesiastical tradition. Instead, they are attuned to the personal experience of the
individual, with the Bible as the sole authority for living the
Christian life. Methodists, for example, know God through
their own efforts; there are no intermediaries.

∎ Fourth, *sectarian churches.* For these, all theology is local.

CREEDS AND CONFESSIONS

Think of creeds as pledges of allegiance. The use of precise professions of the church's beliefs, or creeds, is almost as old as the church itself. According to Tertullian and other sources, the early creed was a token, referring to the ancient practice of one friend's sending a stranger to another friend with an earthenware fragment as a gesture of introduction. Similarly, recital of the creed was one way strangers could make themselves known to other Christians during a time of persecution. But as the church grew, so did theological disputes, and the creed changed to reflect the orthodox beliefs of the church. For the Orthodox, the Niceno-Constantinopolitan or Constantinopolitan Creed is the "symbol" of Orthodox faith; the Roman Catholic church used an eleventh-century variation of the Niceno-Constantinopolitan Creed as its own symbol. There were also many other credal expressions, but they all shared one common characteristic: They each were divided into three parts to discuss the Trinitarian convictions of the church.

No new creeds were developed until the sixteenth century, when the Augsburg Confession explicitly outlined Lutheran dogma. In the following century, other expressions of Protestant belief—notably, the Presbyterian Westminster Confession and the Church of England's Thirty-Nine Articles—were formulated.

THE ONE BOOK I WOULD READ . . .

Anne Morrow Lindbergh's *Gift from the Sea*. It came out at a time when I was living in the suburbs and the only thing that I ever read back then was the manual for my steam iron. It's a small, slim volume, but I read it over and over and over again. I still go back and read it from time to time.

It had an impact on me—it made me search myself and find out what I was all about and where I was going, and about the potential that women have. The other books on the women's movement, *The Feminine Mystique* and all those, didn't do it for me. I found them strident and they didn't relate to me all that much. They certainly didn't contain much spirituality.

I discovered *Gift from the Sea* back in the late fifties or early sixties. I was not a career mom. I had a career early, then had children late, and only after that did I return to writing. But I don't think that *Gift from the Sea* is out of date, even now. I think any young person reading it today would find the same things in it that I did back then.

—Erma Bombeck
columnist and author

CREED CREDENTIALS

NAME	DETAILS
The Old Roman Creed	This early (second century) symbol formed the basis for the Apostles' Creed. It may be traced back to the writings of Bishops Felix and Dionysus (third century) and of Tertullian (second century). I believe in God [the] Father Almighty and in Jesus Christ, His only Son, our Lord, who was born of the Holy Spirit and the Virgin Mary, crucified under Pontius Pilate, and buried; the third day He rose from the dead. He ascended into heaven; he sitteth at the right hand of the Father; thence He shall come to judge living and dead. And in the Holy Ghost, [the] holy Church, [the] remission of sins, [the] resurrection of the flesh.
The Apostles' Creed	For centuries, it was thought that this baptismal creed had been constructed by the Twelve Apostles themselves, with each of them giving one of the creed's lines. In fact, this creed did not appear in the now commonly accepted form until the eighth century. I believe in God the Father Almighty, Maker of heaven and earth; and in Jesus Christ, His only Son, our Lord, who was conceived by the Holy Spirit, born of the Virgin Mary, suffered under Pontius Pilate, was crucified, dead, and buried; He descended into hell; the third day He rose again from the dead. He ascended into heaven and sitteth on the right hand of God the Father Almighty; from thence He shall come to judge the living and the dead. I believe in the Holy

NAME	DETAILS
The Apostles' Creed (cont.)	Ghost, the holy Catholic Church; the Communion of Saints; the forgiveness of sins; the resurrection of the body; and the life everlasting.
The Creed of Eusebius	The Creed of Eusebius was composed c. C.E. 325 in Caesarea and proved highly influential, providing the basis of the creed developed at the first Nicene Council. We believe in one God the Father Almighty, the maker of all things visible and invisible, and in one Lord Jesus Christ, the Word of God, God of God, Light of Light, (Life of Life), only begotten son (firstborn of all creation, before all worlds begotten of God the Father), by whom all things were made, who for our salvation was incarnate (and lived as a citizen amongst men), and suffered, and rose the third day, and ascended (to the Father), and shall come again (in glory) to judge quick and dead. And (we believe) in (one) Holy Ghost.
The Creed of Jerusalem	The Creed of Jerusalem, written, most probably, by Saint Cyril of Jerusalem around C.E. 350, was influential in adapting the first Nicene Creed at the subsequent Council of Constantinople in 381, when the Niceno-Constantinopolitan Creed was finally promulgated. I [*or* we] believe in one God the Father, Almighty, maker of heaven and earth, and of all things visible and invisible. And in one Lord Jesus Christ, the only begotten Son of God, begotten of His Father, very God before all worlds, by whom all things were made; was incarnate, and was made Man, crucified, and buried. (He)

NAME	DETAILS
The Creed of Jerusalem (cont.)	rose again the third day and ascended into heaven and sat on the right hand of the Father and shall come in glory to judge the quick and the dead whose kingdom shall have no end. And in one Holy Spirit, the Paraclete, who spake in the Prophets. And in one baptism of repentance for remission of sins, and in one holy Catholic Church, and in resurrection of the flesh, and in life eternal.
The Creed of Saint Jerome	The Creed of Saint Jerome, although never in widespread use, is seen as important in bridging the concerns of the Eastern and Western churches by inserting phrases from the Jerusalem creed into a version of the baptismal creed.
	I believe in one God the Father Almighty, maker of things visible and invisible. I believe in one Lord Jesus Christ, the Son of God, born of God, God of God, Light of Light, Almighty of Almighty, true God of true God, born before the ages, not made, by whom all things were made in heaven and in earth, who for our salvation descended from heaven; was conceived of the Holy Ghost, born of the Virgin Mary; suffered by suffering under Pontius Pilate, under Herod the king; crucified; buried; descended into hell; trod down the sting of death; rose again; the third day, He appeared to the apostles. After this, He ascended into heaven, sitteth at the right of God the Father, thence shall come to judge the quick and the dead. And I believe in the Holy Ghost, God not unbegotten nor begotten, not created or made, but co-eternal with the Father and the Son. I believe that there is remission of sins in the holy catholic

NAME	DETAILS
The Creed of Saint Jerome (cont.)	church, communion of saints, resurrection of the flesh unto eternal life. Amen.
The Niceno-Constantinopolitan Creed	The Niceno-Constantinopolitan Creed is based on a dogmatic statement formulated at the first ecumenical Council of Nicaea in C.E. 325 to settle the Arian controversy concerning the persons of the Trinity. Then, influenced by the earlier models, it was heavily modified by a subsequent ecumenical Council of Constantinople to reflect with greater clarity the church's beliefs. I believe in one God, the Father Almighty, Maker of heaven and earth, and of all things visible and invisible. And in one Lord Jesus Christ, the Son of God, begotten to the Father before all ages, Light of Light; true God of true God; begotten, not made; of one essence with the Father, by whom all things were made; who, for us men, and for our salvation, came down from the heavens and was incarnate of the Holy Spirit and the Virgin Mary, and became man; and was crucified for us under Pontius Pilate, and suffered, and was buried; and arose again on the third day according to the Scriptures; and sitteth at the right hand of the Father; and shall come again, with glory, to judge both the living and the dead; whose kingdom shall have no end. And in the Holy Spirit, the Lord, the Giver of Life; who proceedeth from the Father; who with the Father and the Son together is worshipped and glorified; who spake by the prophets. In one holy, catholic, and apostolic church. I confess one baptism for the remission of sins. I look for the resurrection of the dead and the life of the age [*or* world] to come. Amen.

NAME	DETAILS
The Athanasian Creed	The Athanasian Creed (*Quicumgue vult*) was written in Gaul between C.E. 420 and 430, and despite its attribution to Saint Athanasius, probably by Saint Hilary of Arles. It begins, "Whoever wants to be saved should above all cling to the Catholic faith. Whoever does not guard it whole and inviolable will doubtless perish eternally. . . ." The author would no doubt be surprised to see it in the *Lutheran Book of Worship* and in other Protestant manuals.
The Augsburg Confession	The Augsburg Confession of Martin Luther considerably rearranged orthodox doctrine and became the basis for further Protestant experimentation.

SACRIFICES, SACRAMENTALS, AND SACRAMENTS

Sacrifices

In Christianity, the sacraments are the main thing. They're not to be confused with the "sacrifices"—although there are some obvious connections, especially since most sacrificial rituals take on a sacramental quality in the religion to which they belong. In the broader context of general religious expression, a sacrifice has several qualifying characteristics:

- *There must be a ritual presentation.* The rite will vary, of course, to suit the reason for making the sacrifice.
- *The thing sacrificed must have a value.* Goats work. So does food. These days, there's a cash equivalency attached to the goats of yore.
- *There must be a reason for making the sacrifice.* General giving isn't really part of this picture. Typically, sacrifices are made to bring rain, grow corn, and win wars. In this sense, sacrifices are a kind of cosmic *baksheesh*. More elevated forms of sacrifice involve giving thanks, making atonement, or achieving communion with a deity.

There are lots of examples of sacrifices in religion; some are humbly spread upon a table for your approval, O Mighty Reader, on the next page.

Sacramentals

Sacramentals differ from sacraments, in Christian theology, because they were not ordained by Christ as part of His teaching. That doesn't mean they aren't sacred activities. Saying the Rosary, fasting, observing holy days, blessing homes, elevating the Cross—many or all these religious gestures are enshrined by the Roman and Orthodox churches and subscribed to partly by the Anglican church and, to an even lesser extent, by the Lutheran church. They are seen as sacred signs of faith but not capable of bestowing grace in and of themselves. It wasn't until the eleventh century that the Western church decided there ought to be a distinction made between *sacraments* and *sacramentals*.

> **A LITTLE RITUAL GOES A LONG WAY**
>
> From a religious point of view, a little ritual is a handy thing. There's nothing like a long-prescribed formula to conjure ancient origins, summon the dignity of tradition, enhance the mystery of faith, and conjure the presence of the departed—not to mention what it does for institutional loyalty. Scientific chaps say there is a strong psychopull to ritual, one that begins in childhood, when routine is rich and required. For details, read C. G. Jung or Sir James George Fraser's *Golden Bough,* mentioned earlier.

Sacraments

The sacraments of the church are those things the faithful believe were instituted by Christ as necessary for salvation. Roman Catholics believe in the necessity of all seven, but in most cases a typical Catholic will experience only six of the seven.

However, the number of sacraments varies from denomination to denomination. Only the Roman Catholic and Orthodox churches accept the necessity of all seven sacraments; most Protestant churches accept the necessity of only baptism and the Eucharist.

> **THE SEVEN SACRAMENTS**
> - Baptism
> - Confirmation
> - Eucharist (Communion)
> - Penance
> - Marriage
> - Ordination
> - Holy unction (a.k.a. last rites, or the anointing of the sick)

FASTING, FAST, FASTER

Among the more personal voluntary sacrifices made for moral and religious purposes, fasting is the one that seems to provide the most direct connection to mysticism and asceticism. For that reason, it is a fairly universal custom, although most religions don't have specifically appointed days or rules of fasting. For those that do, however, fasting is an important aspect of spiritual watchfulness.

- *In Judaism,* the solemn fast appointed to be observed on the tenth day of the seventh month was apparently taken seriously in antiquity, since the penalty for disobedience was death. The rules of Jewish fasting include a special commandment requiring strict abstinence from evening to evening. Fasts were seen to be part of a cycle of fasting and feasting. Before a feast could be celebrated, the sins of the people had to be confessed and expiated. Fasting did the job. In the postexile period, private fasting was endorsed by the pious and encouraged by the religious sentiment of the time. Weekly fasts were observed on the second and fifth day of each week, in commemoration of the ascent and descent of Moses at Mount Sinai. The dietary laws of Judaism may be considered a form of fasting.
- *In Christianity,* scholars with appetites have noted that Jesus never commanded a fast for any reason—although it's likely that He obeyed contemporary Jewish customs, and it is mentioned that He once fasted for 40 days and nights. But the sacrificial emphasis of Christian theology and the spiritual focus on anticipation of the Second Coming made fasting a natural discipline in the early church. The apostles, for example, frequently fasted.

  Roman Catholic practice no longer requires keeping a weekly fast, although certain Lenten periods are still indicated as fast days when only fish may be eaten.

  Orthodox practice requires fasting two days each week—Wednesdays and Fridays—and during many days during the year as the church proceeds through its cycle of feasts and fasts. In Orthodoxy, fasting means abstaining from eggs, dairy, meat, fish, and olive oil, although some Orthodox consider fish to be acceptable. As in most matters of Orthodox discipline, the faithful are encouraged to keep the rules but are generally not judged by others if they are neglectful. Orthodoxy also has a tradition of fasting from the flesh—abstaining from sex—during certain times. Married priests, for instance, are required to abstain before celebrating the Divine Liturgy.

  Protestant practice leaves fasting completely to the individual, although the Westminster Confession (Presbyterian) requires fasting one day each week, a custom long ago discarded.
- *In Islam,* the month of Ramadan, in which the first part of the Koran is said to have been received, is by command of the prophet observed as a period of strict fasting. No food or drink of any kind is permitted to be taken from daybreak until full

nightfall. Ramadan is often a very warm month, making denial of water a difficult personal task. There are not many other fasting days on the Moslem calendar, but most devout Moslems agree that Ramadan's enough for the whole year, even though Muhammad himself called fasting the "gate of religion," and forbade it only on the two great festivals, that which immediately follows Ramadan and that which succeeds the pilgrimage to Mecca.

SACRIFICIAL SINGULARITIES	
SACRIFICERS	**SACRIFICED**
Greeks	Farmyard animals, especially goats. The animals were roasted, then consumed as a way of attaining oneness with the gods—a Greco-religio version of "you are what you eat," one supposes.
Aztecs, Incas, Toltecs	People—and lots of them. Most historians believe Aztec sacrifices polished off as many as 20,000 people a year. Back then, it was "you are what the gods eat."
Hindus	People, plants, animals—although after the earliest period of Hinduism, this practice was largely abandoned.
Chinese	Ancient Chinese. In later periods, people were replaced as sacrificial offerings by food and animals. This seems only suitable, since many sacrifices were offered to ancestors.
Buddhists	Incense, candles, flowers.
Jews	Goats again. Early on, Yom Kippur was a very bad day for goats, which were invested with the collective and individual sins of the people, then tossed off Jerusalem's walls as a gesture of atonement. After the destruction of the Temple at Jerusalem (C.E. 70), sacrificial rituals became largely symbolic.
Christians	God. Talk about a table turner. In Christian theology, Christ as God sacrificed Himself for humankind.

BAPTISM

The business of giving newcomers to a cult or religion a ritual cleansing isn't a purely Christian novelty, as the early church fathers were well aware. Tertullian (C.E. 155–222, more or less), the Solzhenitsyn of the early church, talked about damp initiation rites not only of the followers of Isis and Mithras but also of those adepts in pursuit of the mysteries of Apollo and Eleusis. For millennia, Jews had performed ritual absolutions. The shared motive, according to Tertullian, was the belief that the water carried away guilt and granted a "regeneration and exemption" from previous wrongdoing. Nevertheless, the rebirth symbolized by the Christian baptism is unique, contributing as much to other traditions as it borrowed from them. During those days, as Frederick Cornwallis Conybeare once wrote:

> The idea of rebirth was in the air; it was the very keynote of all the solemn initiations and mysteries—Mithraic, Orphic, Eleusinian—through which repentant pagans secured pardon and eternal bliss. Yet there is not much evidence that the Church directly borrowed many of its ceremonies or interpretations from outside sources. They for the most part originated among believers, and not improbably the outside cults borrowed as much from the Church as it from them.

In Christian theology, baptism and the Eucharist are the two principal redemptive sacraments.

Trinitarian Formula

The formula for baptism is ancient; it's described in the Didache, one of the earliest Christian documents extant:

1. Now concerning baptism, thus baptize ye: Having spoken beforehand all these things, baptize into the name of the Father and of the Son and of the Holy Spirit, in living water.
2. But if thou hast not living water, baptize into other water; if thou canst not in cold, in warm.
3. But if thou hast not either, pour water upon the head thrice, in the name of the Father and of the Son and of the Holy Spirit.
4. Now before the baptism, let him that is baptizing and him that is being baptized fast, and any others who can; but thou

biddest him who is being baptized to fast one or two days before.

THE ONE BOOK I WOULD READ . . .

At the risk of sounding biblically irreverent, I have come to regard Dostoyevsky's *The Brothers Karamazov* as the "fifth gospel." This novel not only wrestles honestly and relentlessly with the spiritual dimensions of the fallen human race; it also provides a distinctly Orthodox Christian vision of redeemed humanity in the best New Testament tradition of voluntary suffering, unlimited love, and universal forgiveness. It is the quintessential novel of resurrection.

> —Father Alexander F. C. Webster
> parish priest, St. Mary's Orthodox Church (OCA), Falls Church, Virginia
> author of *The Price of Prophecy:*
> *Orthodox Churches on Peace, Freedom, and Security*

I think it would be a novel—Dostoyevsky's *The Brothers Karamazov*. I'm not sure that's the book for everybody, of course. But it's a picture of life lived intensely but at the same time also philosophically.

The Brothers Karamazov brings out different points of view—sensual, intellectual, religious—on how life should be lived. And these conflicts are not just abstract but embodied in people. It's really a panorama of life that I've not seen matched in any other book I've picked up.

The book frames the world in terms of the brothers or their father. One sees aspects of them in everything and because they're three brothers and a father—which is a very important factor; it means they're not separated from each other—they are not only in conflict but they are also aspects of each other.

The idea in *The Brothers Karamazov* is that the world always—and people always—present themselves to you under multiple aspects. This includes myself. When I see myself, I see the multiple aspects of different ways to relate to the world and other people—selfish, sad, forgiving, cynical, and so forth.

> —Kenneth J. Arrow
> winner of the Nobel Prize for economics, 1972

The things "spoken beforehand" are the moral precepts known as the two ways—the way of life and the way of death—with which the Didache begins. The Didache itself was written circa C.E. 100, but the things "spoken beforehand" part of the document almost certainly predates the rest and is probably from the eighth decade C.E.

Saint Justin Martyr describes baptism in his *Apology for the Christians,* written around C.E. 140:

I will . . . relate the manner in which we dedicated ourselves to God when we had been made new by Christ. As many as are persuaded and believe that what we teach and say is true, and undertake to be able to live accordingly, are instructed to pray and entreat God with fasting, for the remission of their sins are past, we praying and fasting with them. Then they are brought by us where there is water, and are regenerated in the same manner in which we were ourselves regenerated. For in the name of God, the Father and Lord of the universe, and of our Savior Jesus Christ and of the Holy Spirit, they then receive the washing with water. . . .

There is pronounced over him who chooses to be born again, and has repented of his sins, the name of God the Father and Lord of the universe, he who leads to the laver the person that is to be washed calling Him by this name alone. For no one can utter the name of the ineffable God, and this washing is called Illuminations, because they who learn these things are illuminated in their understandings. And in the name of Jesus Christ, who was crucified under Pontius Pilate, and in the name of the Holy Ghost, who through the prophets foretold all things about Jesus, he who is illuminated is washed.

Saint Justin Martyr (circa C.E. 100–164) was born in Flavia Neapolis, in what is now the West Bank, and spent most of his youth reading philosophical works by Greeks and the Stoics. When he stumbled upon the books of the Hebrew Bible and the New Testament, he found himself converted to Christianity, in whose cause he died under Emperor Marcus Aurelius, refusing to honor the state religion. The highly valuable insights he provides about the earliest days of the church are found in his two-volume *Apologies for the Christians,* available in several translations. His only other known work is the *Dialogue with Trypho,* which contains useful comparisons of Christianity and Judaism in the second century.

For many years during the church's earliest period, baptism was regularly called "illumination."

Late in the second century, Tertullian described the rite of baptism in his treatises *On Baptism* and *On the Resurrection of the Flesh.* According to him, a typical baptism, after a period of fasting and prayer, went like this:

1. Initiates were baptized to free their souls from the strain of sinfulness.
2. The initiates were anointed with holy oil to consecrate their souls.
3. They were then "sealed"—signed with the Cross—to protect their souls.

4. The bishop then laid hands on initiates to illuminate their souls with the Holy Spirit.
5. The Eucharist was celebrated.
6. After baptism, the initiates were given a drink of milk and honey.

Other Methods of Baptizing

Not all baptisms followed the Trinitarian formula, and by the third century, so many were being baptized in the name of Jesus alone that Pope Stephen I was forced to declare that formula valid. By the fifth century, however, the three persons of the Trinity were once again invoked nearly universally—with Armenia being the most notable of several regional exceptions.

By the end of Christianity's third century, baptism had certain fixed elements:

- Most baptisms were performed at Easter, although Pentecost and the feast of Epiphany were also used as fasts for receiving catechumens.
- Catechumens announced their desire to become members of the church by giving their names to the local bishop.
- They were given a catechetic course explaining the principal tenants of the faith, after which they were questioned by clerics to ensure the converts had a complete understanding of the church's beliefs.
- They were given repeated exorcisms to achieve a certain spiritual hygiene.
- They were given the creed to memorize.
- They were "sealed" with sanctified oil.
- Facing west, they pronounced a renunciation of the Devil; then facing east, they pronounced the creed they had memorized.
- The water in the font was exorcised, then blessed. The converts then stepped into the font. Many were not immersed but simply had water poured over them by the presiding cleric, who pronounced the baptismal formula: "I baptize thee in the name of the Father and the Son and the Holy Spirit."

OTHER FORMS OF RITUAL PURIFICATION

Virtually every culture has a way of taking out the stains of daily living. The main culprits: birth, death, and bloodshed—and especially that pesky menstrual blood. Some rites of purification are elegant, whereas others are frankly in need of a little purification themselves. A small list of solvents:

- *Annual renewal rituals involving bloodletting.* Aztecs loved this stuff. Followers of the cult of Mithras used to drench themselves in ox blood.
- *Vicarious sacrifices,* such as the ritual slaughter of a lamb or goat, as once practiced in Jerusalem, or the firing of the manager, as practiced at Yankee Stadium.
- *Washing with the urine of a sacred cow.* India. But then what?
- *Fumigation with incense.* Along with abstention from sex, confession, and fasting, this is a fairly standard mainstream purification gambit. Among some tribes in Nilotic Africa, the cleansing smoke is made from burning cow dung.
- *Sprinkling.* In Armenia, fields and flocks are sprinkled with holy water.
- *Hang-dog expressions.* In Zoroastrianism, demons infecting a corpse can be driven off by a look from certain kinds of dogs.

- They were anointed at various places on their bodies with scented oil—called chrism—by deacons if they were male and by deaconesses if they were female.
- They donned white garments.
- They were given the sign of the cross on their foreheads.
- They were given a first communion, often with milk and honey added to the host.

To Dunk or Not to Dunk?

The baptism-by-immersion element is generally a red-flag issue for traditionalists—both fundamentalists and Orthodox—but archaeological evidence suggests that infusion—the pouring on of water—may have been a widespread practice during the church's earliest years, since most of the fonts uncovered have been much too small to accommodate the complete believer. The Jewish ceremony of ablution, however, required the water to run away from the believer, and this was—and still is—the requirement in almost all Christian baptisms as well.

"Living Water"

Most early Church authorities agreed that baptisms were best performed in bodies of running waters—rivers and streams. But many were baptized in lakes, and many more were baptized in shallow fonts. Tertullian writes, "It makes no difference whether one is washed in the sea or in a pool, in a river or spring, in a lake or a ditch. Nor can we distinguish between those whom John [the Baptist] baptized in the Jordan and those whom Peter baptized in the Tiber." The Didache says "to pour water on the head" and leaves it at that, but most religious art for the first millennium of the church's existence shows initiates standing in the water while water is poured over their heads from a bowl or from the hand of the presiding cleric. Early manuscripts contain rubrics calling for total immersion, but that was not a widespread practice until at least after the eighth century.

> ▪ *Snot.* Among primitive peoples, this stuff works: spitting and blowing the nose, getting bitten by swarms of ants, branding and tattooing, knocking out teeth.

Godparents

Originally, parents could sponsor their own children—although the practice was outlawed by the Roman Catholic church in the ninth century—and the number of godparents occasionally exceeded the number of parishioners. By the seventeenth century, however, the number of godparents had been restricted to two—one from each sex. (Anglican churches allow *three.*) These days, even Marlon Brando can be a godfather; in fact, Pop's drinking buddies down at the Oasis Lounge can all stand up as godfathers to a new kid. But, at least to Catholics and Orthodox Christians, there are still requirements for the job—and neither children nor grown-up catechumens can be baptized without the presence of at least one approved sponsor.

For a Roman Catholic perspective, read Karl Rahner's *Foundations of Christian Faith: An Introduction to the Idea of Christianity.*

THE EUCHARIST

The central act of Christian worship is the communion service variously

> **THE GODPARENTAL JOB DESCRIPTION**
>
> ▪ Sponsors have to guarantee that their godchild will have a healthy religious life, with plenty of nutritional religious instruction added in the event the child's parents die or fail to offer religious guidance themselves.
> ▪ Nonmembers of the church need not apply, since they are by definition unqualified to teach the child about religion.
> ▪ Also disqualified: people who are leading lives of sin. This stricture, however, does not disqualify politicians.

THE MYSTERY OF THE BREAD AND WINE

To Christians, the Eucharistic service is full of mystery and miracles in which the bread and the wine assume different qualities, depending on the denomination.

▪ *Transubstantiation:* The belief that the "accidents"—an Aristotelian term used to describe the visible characteristics of the bread and wine—are transformed by consecration into their real essences—the body and blood of Christ. In Roman Catholicism, the Host is offered to the congregation in one "kind"—as wafers of unleavened bread. The wine is reserved for the priest.

The term *transubstantiation* is unknown in Orthodox dogmatic theology, although the belief is the same—that the bread and wine are transformed into the body and blood of Christ. The Orthodox refer to this simply as a "mystery," a term first used in the early church to describe the miracle, and one that is redolent of other "mysteries," notably the Eleusinian ones practiced in Greece until the fourth century C.E. The Orthodox serve the Host from a chalice in which leavened bread, wine, and warm water have been mixed. Communicants take the Host from a small spoon offered by the priest.

▪ *Consubstantiation:* A theory developed by Martin Luther, who maintained that although the elements of the Eucharist are transformed into the body and blood of Christ, they also maintain their original "accidents."

▪ *Virtualism:* Presbyterians and some other Protestant denominations believe that although the elements are not changed, consecration does confer the "power" of Christ's body and blood.

▪ *Memorialism:* Many Protestants simply believe the communion service is a commemorative event, recalling Christ's life and passion.

Roger T. Beckwith's *Priesthood and Sacraments; A Study in the Anglican–Methodist Report* discusses the Anglican and Methodist views of all this, whereas Joseph Martos's *Doors to the Sacred: A Historical Introduction to Sacraments in the Catholic Church* explores the Catholic sense of the sacraments.

described as the Mass (Catholic), the Divine Liturgy (Orthodox), or the Lord's Supper (Protestant). The event commemorated is the final meal shared by Christ and his disciples, during which, according to the Scriptures, he blessed the bread and wine, calling them his body and his blood. That's about all Christians can agree on; beyond that, they splinter, by denomination, over the nature of the ritual and its meaning.

Most Catholic and Orthodox theologians consider the communion service to be at once sacrificial and redemptive. Protestants generally subscribe to the notion that Christ's "spirit" is recalled during the communion. This divergence is reflected in liturgical practices: Orthodox Divine Liturgies are ornate and ancient; they're longer than most other services, and they're chanted by the priest, deacon, choir, and congregation, without musical accompaniment. Catholic Masses are more straightforward—in fact, since the Second Vatican Council, they have often been starkly Protestant in character—but they nonetheless reflect the traditional structure of the ritual, directed, as it is, toward the central Eucharistic celebration. Protestant churches vary from the liturgical conventions of Lutheranism and Anglicanism, with echoes of their Roman Catholic provenance, to the relatively formless services of the Quakers, where both liturgy and sacraments are unknown.

Among those denominations who celebrate the communion service, the ritual is usually preceded by a penitential gesture or sacrament, in the case of the Catholic and Orthodox churches, where it is commonly called confession. In Protestant churches, confession is usually made by the entire congregation at once, if at all. In Roman Catholicism and Orthodoxy, confessions are made privately and in confidence, before a priest granted the authority, by his bishop, to hear confessions. An Orthodox priest witnesses the confession; a Catholic priest assumes the person of Christ and offers absolution.

Confession has changed over the life of the church. In the ante-Nicene church, confessions were generally heard only once in a lifetime—sometimes in front of the whole congregation, sometimes on a deathbed, after a lifetime of saving up postbaptismal transgressions. But in the thirteenth century, when the laity was encouraged to participate in the Eucharist more frequently, the Western church began requiring confession at least once a year. In the Eastern church, where, until relatively recently, taking communion was a fairly rare occurrence—no matter how often a believer attended services—penance also was consequently infrequent.

MARRIAGE

Many gods, many wives. One God, one wife—everywhere except in Islam, whose practice of polygamy is slowly withering.

Christian Marriage

Christian marriage, in the Roman Catholic and Orthodox churches, is a sacrament, which, for practical purposes, means that when you say, "I do," you're making the same handshake with God you make with your partner. In those two ancient churches, marriage and ordination to holy orders are the only sacramental events you can actually plan for yourself; baptism's too early in life's morning for sentient thought, whereas sacraments for the mortally ill are generally in somebody else's hands.

The primary goal of a Christian marriage is to create a church-sanctioned partnership for the nurturing of children and the establishment of a family. Although many Protestant churches accept divorce as unfortunate, they generally accept secular law and permit remarriage in the church to those previously married. The Catholic and Orthodox churches don't have as lenient a view of marriage.

In the Roman Catholic church, divorce is not permitted. However, annulments may be granted in some instances. Most non-Catholics assume those instances must involve marital infidelity or abuse or something similar. In fact, the grounds for a Catholic annulment are generally based on other factors. Especially relevant to church authorities is whether both partners were aware of the sacramental nature of a marriage, inside or outside the church.

In the Orthodox church, bishops may dissolve a marriage on generally the same grounds; Orthodoxy also provides for a second marriage, although in tone and language the ceremony is repentant, rather than triumphant.

The Anglican church also has an official position forbidding divorce, but it is very rarely enforced, especially recently.

Marriage in all Christian churches is also the basis for enshrining sexual activity within the limits of chastity. In dogmatic theology, to be chaste is not the same as to be celibate. Chastity applies to the virtuous pursuit of a sexual relationship as part of a marriage. Roman Catholic priests, for example, are bound by promises of chastity, not celibacy. But since marriage is forbidden to those in Roman Catholic orders, chastity is equated with celibacy.

> **THE CHURCH ON WOMEN IN MARRIAGE**
>
> Despite recent politically correct cant, the history of the church may be more or less described by its dedication to protecting women within the shelter of a marriage, the sanctity of which is perpetually guaranteed by the church. "Deadbeat dads" have been a longtime fear of the church. For a history of church–family relations, start with Frances and Joseph Gies's *Marriage and Family in the Middle Ages*.

Jewish Marriage

Jewish marriage customs reflect the same basic ambitions as those in Christian customs: Jews are obliged to marry and, according to Talmudic law, to bear at least two children, one boy and one girl. More is good. None is bad. The overriding rule here is the explicit instruction given by God in Genesis to "be fruitful and multiply." The marriage ceremony itself is essentially benedictional—in fact, the marriage service, conducted under a canopy called a *chuppah*—involves a blessing over wine and the pronouncement of seven wedding benedictions.

Divorce in Judaism is the subject of a religious ceremony, in which the husband must present to his wife a formal document of divorce.

Islamic Marriage

Islamic marriage, in contrast to the Jewish and Christian traditions, is largely a secular agreement. The nonsacramental aspect of Islamic marriage accounts for the growing secularization of marital customs, in which childhood betrothals and polygamous unions are disappearing under the weight of modern civil laws.

Divorce is the right of men only in Islam. Although this, too, has begun to erode, unilateral divorce at will by the husband still has the authority of the *Shariá,* the Islamic code of law and behavior.

LAST WORDS

The last sacrament is last rites or extreme (or holy) unction (neither term is currently used, by the way), or, more euphemistically, the anointing of the sick. Very sick. Then comes the funeral—sad, but no sacrament.

Good thing people die, or we'd never know anything about how they lived. Mausoleums are rough museums filled with the evidence that when it comes to the end of the line, we all step onto the same platform of uncertainty.

Funeral rites, since the first bite of cosmic dust, have all included certain key characteristics:

- *The assumption that a dead body is a dirty body.* While we're alive, we love touching, fondling, kissing each other. But as the soul flees, a taboo attaches to the corpse, and even the briefest touch has always been considered unclean. Even the thought of a touch is considered unclean. Even typing that sentence . . .
- *Mourning.* Funny, but sadness has a long history associated with funerals.
- *Formal arrangements.* The appointments of death chambers or an elaborate formality in the position of the body all suggest a universal sense of post-life prep.
- *An attempt to establish a communion with the dead.* Usually this is done in a funeral feast, ceremony, wake, or something similar. In southeast Asia, this correspondence can last a long, long time, since dead people are sometimes lodged in the walls of their kids' houses. On a more secular level, the writer knows of an Appalachian farmer whose wife died in late June, but she was simply shut up in the bedroom until, in early August, the undertaker was finally called. Why the delay? Social Security payments. "I hate it when they do this in the middle of the summer," said the undertaker. A similar sentiment is expressed

in greatly exaggerated form by James Joyce in *Finnegans Wake*.

■ *A ceremony or sacrifice for the dead,* along with prayers for the forgiveness of their sins or for the peaceful repose of their souls.

■ *Death witchery.* Now, *there's* a phrase. According to Mary H. Kingsley (*West African Studies*), 60 percent of the deaths in Africa at the turn of the twentieth century were due to "witchcraft and sorcery." Here's how it worked: Since most tribesmen had a sort of experiential relationship with health, their assumption was that death could be caused only by old age, severe trauma, or loss of blood. Anything else—and that included most diseases—was obviously the fault of magical curses. The job of the witch doctor was to figure out who had placed the curse on the dead person. Every African postmortem, therefore, involved the murder of the person—or persons—who caused the death of the sick person. The modern preoccupation with causes of death mirrors this earlier, more primitive fascination.

■ *The need to protect the dead from demons.* Many people believed that a dying person's last gasp was the sweetest sound a demon could hear, so the rituals and traditions that once served to protect the body and soul from demonic possession were rich and varied, start-

---

SAYING SAYONARA

There are lots of ways of giving a last long good-bye to a departed friend or relative. Here are three:

■ *The Hindu practice* involves a procession to the crematorium led by a chief mourner carrying a torch. Just before the body is committed to the fire, the funeral procession circles the bier. If a widow was determined to commit suttee—in which she threw herself on the fire—this was the time to do it.

■ *A servant's work is never done.* Many civilizations assumed that one of the things a rich man could take with him was his servants. This practice—prevalent in ancient Egypt, Greece, and in parts of Asia (especially China)—concerned the help not a little, but as it was assumed that their master would need their attention in the next world, just as he had in this one, they went along with the funeral.

■ *Jewish funerals* are followed by a week-long period of seclusion and mourning—called shivah—by the remaining members of the family.

Elisabeth Kübler-Ross's *On Death and Dying* is the standard book of the dead, treating the psychological dimension of the event. Jessica Mitford's magnificent *The American Way of Death* offers the aspiring funeral planner a great deal of inside info. D. J. Enright compiled *The Oxford Book of Death,* a lively collection of morbid observations by Evelyn Waugh, James Joyce, and many others.

ing with the final exhalation of life. It was a common medieval belief that if a bell were sounded at the moment of death, it would banish unseen ghouls hovering around the corpse, intent on nabbing the dead person's fleeing soul as it sprinted to heaven.

In Christian funeral rites, many prayers were once for the protection of the body from violation by vampires—hence the solid construction of some ancient tombs. It was the desire to ward off the assaults of demons that gave rise to the customs of sealing the coffin with the Cross, lighting candles around a dead body, and keeping a coffinside vigil through the night. The consecrated bread of the Eucharist was often buried with believers. Saint Basil is said to have specially consecrated a Host to be placed in his coffin.

It was probably the fear of demonic assaults on the dead that inspired the somewhat unhygienic custom of burying dead people under the floors of churches, and as near as possible to the altar. In the Orthodox Church, this practice was happily forbidden by the Justinian Code. Saint Ephrem Syrus, in his testament, particularly commanded that his body not be laid inside a church. As a consequence, he was left alone outside.

- *Protection of the living from the dead.* Just-in-case fear of ghosts is one explanation for the early appeal of cremation. The cleanup factor is the other. Barrows, earth mounds, rock crypts—all these primitive mausoleums contain big piles of burned bones. But the taboo associated with corpses shouldn't be confused with the fear of ghosts and other reckless spirits. A corpse is buried or burned or scaffolded on a tree, a tower, or a housetop, according to Professor Frederick Cornwallis Conybeare, to get it out of the way and shield society from potentially dangerous infection. But ghosts in and of themselves need not be feared; at least to most primitive peoples, a kinsman's ghost usually is not. "On the contrary, it is fed and consoled with everything it needs, is asked not to go away but to stay, and is in a thousand ways assured of the sorrow and sympathy of the survivors," wrote Conybeare. Cannibals seem to have actually looked forward to a little haunting, especially when feeling peckish: When the body was eaten, the soul of the deceased was kept inside the family circle.

Strabo (63 B.C.E. to C.E. 25), the Greek geographer and historian, asserts that the ancient Irish regarded it as a high honor to be consumed by relatives. The custom continues, figuratively speaking. In other early societies, relics were the thing: A stash of arrowheads and bones represented the spirit of the dead man. So for primitive peoples, the ghosts you know are not the same as the ghosts you don't know.

> **A PRAYER FROM THE ARMENIAN RITE**
>
> Preserve, Almighty Lord, this man's spirit with all saints and with lovers of Thy holy name. And do Thou seal and guard the sepulcher of Thy servant, Thou who shuttest up the depths and sealest them with Thy almighty right hand . . . so let the seal of Thy Lordship abide unmoved upon this man's sacred dwelling place and upon the shrine which guards Thy servant. And let not any filthy and unclean devil dare to approach him such as assail the body and souls of the heathen, who possess not the birth of the holy font, and have not the dread seal laid upon their graves.

That's certainly not how it is today, of course, when any poltergeist is a ghost-bustable, anti-Casperian kind of thing. It's the possibility of encountering unhappy spirits that keeps most sensible people out of graveyards at night. In some cities, though, such as Cairo, the older cemeteries have been "repurposed," as today's spin doctors say, so the vast neighborhood of tombs built by the Mamelukes to house their dead (the strange necropolis of Cairo) now provides refuge for the city's homeless, while the pyramids—nothing more than high-rise graveyards, really—along with other tomb attractions, provide amusement for Egypt's tourists.

> Strabo planned a vast, 43-volume supplement to the histories of Polybius, but only small chunks of the work exist today. But Strabo's *Geography,* source of the early Irish cannibalism rite mentioned above, is still around.

PROTESTING PROTESTANTS

If, in Protestantism, the sacraments are generally held to be symbolic—

where they are held at all: neither the Quakers nor the Salvation Army accept any sacraments whatsoever—there also are large degrees of difference over most other theological doctrines as well. Sometimes these differences divide various Protestant denominations. But sometimes, they distinguish individual congregations inside a denomination. For instance, there are quite a good many kinds of Baptists.

VARIATIONS ON A BAPTIST HYMN

- American Baptist Association
- American Baptist Churches in the USA
- Baptist Bible Fellowship International
- Baptist General Conference
- Baptist Missionary Association of America
- Bethel Ministerial Association
- Conservative Baptist Association of America
- General Conference of the Evangelical Baptist Church, Inc.
- Landmark Baptists
- National Baptist Evangelical Life and Soul Saving Assembly of the U.S.A.
- Russian Ukraine Evangelical Baptist Union, USA, Inc.
- National Primitive Baptist Convention of the U.S.A.
- North American Baptist Conference
- Union of Latvian Baptists in America
- Primitive Baptists
- Czechoslovak Baptist Convention of the USA/Canada
- Reformed Baptists
- Separate Baptists in Christ (General Association of Separate Baptists)
- Lott Carey Baptist Foreign Mission Convention, USA
- National Baptist Convention, USA, Inc.
- National Baptist Convention of America
- Progressive National Baptist Convention, Inc.
- National Missionary Baptist Convention of America
- Central Baptist Association
- Duck River (and Kindred) Associations of Baptists (Baptist Church of Christ)
- Free Will Baptists
- National Association of Free Will Baptists
- General Association of Regular Baptist Churches
- General Association of General Baptists

- Seventh Day Baptist General Conference, USA and Canada
- Southern Baptist Convention
- Cooperative Baptist Fellowship
- Two-Seed-in-the-Spirit Predestinarian Baptists
- United Baptists
- United Free Will Baptists

The Disneyland of Christian theology has many adventure-filled kingdoms. To begin your own exploration, start with the *Handbook of Denominations in the United States,* by Frank S. Mead, revised by Samuel S. Hill.

THE FIVE CLASSIC ARGUMENTS FOR THE EXISTENCE OF GOD

Believers can never wholly convince skeptics, of course, since the object of their belief eludes objective verification. That has not prevented philosophers and theologians from making energetic efforts to establish, without dispute, the reality of God. Toward that end, five distinct traditions have emerged during the course of the Christian era:

1. **If God is perfect, He must exist. Otherwise, He wouldn't be perfect.** This is the ontological argument advanced by René Descartes and others. An ontological argument is classified as *a priori,* or, literally, "before the fact." An *a priori* argument can be used to classify, from a logical point of view, either a statement or an argument.

SECTARIANS

Sectarians—Pentecostal and evangelical churches—might also be called radical and militant, theologically speaking, since often they reject as corrupt or invalid most beliefs other than their own. As with the Baptists, there is wide variety among different churches, but all are committed to perfect revelation through the Bible and/or through the experience of the Holy Spirit. The Bible remains the infallible Word of God, not to be read in any critical-text way. Sectarians make a distinction between God's truth and all other truth.

In logic, a *statement* is the use of language to say something that is either true or false, such as "God certainly must exist." An *argument,* on the other hand, is a series of statements, called premises, from which another statement—called the conclusion—may follow. With statements, we need to ask whether they are true or false; with arguments, we need to ask whether they are valid or invalid.

A statement or argument is said to be *a priori* if it is a deductive statement—that is, if its truth or falsity (for a statement) or its validity or invalidity (for an argument) can be established without consulting experience. For example, the following is a statement that we can assume to be true without direct experience: *Red = red.* This is the *principle of identity,* one of the bases on which language works because we all agree on fundamentals. *Today is either Monday, Tuesday, Wednesday, Thursday, Friday, Saturday, or Sunday.* This is a tautology, a statement which exhausts all possibilities, and is therefore true. *A hen is a female chicken.* This is a simple definition. We can also know a statement is false *a priori,* as in *Red is both red and blue.* For more of this sort of introduction to logic, see *An Introduction to Logic and Scientific Method,* by Morris R. Cohen and Ernest Nagel (1934). Books on logic published since 1975—and especially those employing "tableaux"—are almost useless.

How to understand an ontological proof: Try Saint Anselm's approach. First, try to say "that than which nothing greater can be conceived" without reading it, so you actually understand it as an idea. Now, let *X* stand for the idea "that than which nothing greater can be conceived." Next, assume that *X* is an idea that exists only in your head. Gotcha. Anselm claimed that which exists in reality is greater than that which is only in your head. So, there is *something* greater than *X,* if, that is, *X* exists only in your head. And that *something* is not only a concept, it is real; it exists in reality—like an idea or like a sentence printed in ink on a page. Therefore, *X* exists in reality. If you deny *X* is real, or say *X* is only in your mind, you are contradicting yourself. God is *X*.

This kind of proof is known as a *reductio ad absurdum*, and it'll give you a headache after a while, since it consists of showing how making a certain assumption lands you in a contradiction. So you have to replace that assumption by its opposite. The assumption—"that which nothing greater can be conceived"—exists only in your mind. By rejecting it, you end up with the opposite—it must exist in reality, and not only as a concept.

Anselm (1033–1109) served as an archbishop of Canterbury, and was at least as irritating to the Norman usurpers as a later archbishop of Canterbury, Saint Thomas à Becket. His arguments appear in both his *Proslogion* and *Liber Gaunilonis pro insipiente.*

2. **Something started this big cosmic ball rolling, so whatever It is, let's call It God.** This is the cosmological argument used by Saint Thomas Aquinas, who thought that reality must have a "first cause." A cosmological argument is classified as *a posteriori,* or "after the fact." Statements whose truth or falsity is established by an appeal to experience are *a posteriori* statements. Characteristically, *a posteriori* statements (or arguments, for that matter) start with facts of experience and reach a conclusion that intends to explain those facts.

Aquinas actually gave separate arguments for the existence of God; three are considered the cosmological proofs. His cosmological arguments derive from the following observations:

- Things change. When something changes, it is changed by something. That thing is also changed by something. One may put these changes together in a series. Aquinas says there cannot be an infinite regress—that at some point one arrives at the first changer that is itself eternally unchanged. That's God.

- Things have reasons or causes for their existence. This argument is essentially a restatement of the preceding argument—that there cannot be an infinite regression of causes, and that the first cause is God.
- Things come into existence and go out of existence, so they do not need to exist. Things do not need to exist because they change. The only thing that needs to exist is God, because there has to be a First Cause, or an Unchanging Changer.

Aquinas adapted Aristotle to suit his needs. The result is a somewhat distant, theoretical God.

Thomas Aquinas is perhaps the most influential theologian in the history of Christianity. His careful modification of "natural theology"—which held that one could come to know God by deliberate, rational thought—with the corrective of divine revelation resulted in a far-reaching and highly effective means of approaching Christian theology. His defense of natural theology can be found in his *Summa Contra Gentiles,* while his further thoughts can be found in his unfinished masterpiece, *Summa Theologica.* Frederick Charles Copleston's *Aquinas* can help sort out this important theologian's contributions.

3. **Creation is such a delicately engineered machine, it must have an intelligent force guiding its conception.** This is the teleological argument favored by William Paley, an influential eighteenth-century Anglican theologian. Teleology is the study of last causes. Its arguments are based on degrees and design.

The degree argument is simple and logical: Something is good, something is better, something is *best.* The maximum of anything is the cause of that thing. We call that cause God.

The design argument is the most popular—and as might be expected, the silliest. Let's say you're a guy at the beach with a significant other and the sun is coming up over the horizon, or going down over the horizon, depending which beach you are at, and she turns, her eyes alight, and says, "Isn't it beautiful? Don't you feel everything fits together in nature?" And you smile. That's the design argument. Of course, even if there is a design in nature, that doesn't prove God exists. It means that there is the possibility that there is a powerful designer in the world. He might be a very large guy with a very white beard, who likes to help guys seduce women at the beach, but it doesn't, like the other arguments, imply that he is omnipotent or infinite or any of those larger than large words we use to signify God.

For more on teleology and religion, see Thomas Minor's *Design Theology.*

4. **Without God, we can't be good—that is, not just well behaved or pleasant or polite, but *really* good, saintly good, Mother Teresa–style good, *damn* good.** This is Immanuel Kant's moral argument, that good behavior must ultimately point toward the existence of God. This argument faded for a while—perhaps owing to a temporary shortage of good behavior during much of the twentieth century—but is now on the comeback trail.

5. **You just know something's gotta be out there: You've thought about it, and thought about it, and now you're *sure* of it.** This is the experiential argument offered by modern theologians like A. E. Taylor and John Baillie.

Professor Baillie's relevant book is *The Experience of God.*

You may notice a singular lack of scientific methodology here, since God apparently prefers to be accepted on faith, one way or another. Perhaps He feels that if you can't believe the hard way, you don't deserve to believe at all.

You may also note a gender preference here in discussing God. We've used "He," but it's unlikely that God has a sexual identity. Feel free, therefore, to grab another suitable pronoun. In Christian Orthodox theology, God is "pure spirit."

WHO'S IN CHARGE IN HEAVEN

Even assuming God does exist, that alone is not sufficient reason to also believe that heaven and immortality are part of the package. After all, if God was *not* invented by us, what does He owe us?

DANTE'S CELESTIAL HIERARCHY

In heaven, the administrative details have already been worked out. Surprisingly, the big personnel office in the sky is wonderfully streamlined. Here, according to Dante, is the career ladder upstairs, but in descending order:

RANK	JOB DESCRIPTION
1. *Seraphim*	Glorification of God
2. *Cherubim*	Glorification of God
3. *Thrones*	Regulation of the duties of the angels
4. *Dominions*	Regulation of the duties of the angels
5. *Virtues*	Generation and coordination of all miracles on Earth
6. *Powers*	Protection of humankind from all demons
7. *Archangels*	Ministers and guardians to men and women
8. *Principalities*	Ministers and guardians to men and women
9. *Angels*	Ministers and guardians to men and women

Obviously, only a handful of jobs in heaven are filled by seraphim and cherubim. Few are stronger than their powers, even fewer exceed their virtues, and almost nobody rises above their thrones. As in heaven, so on Earth.

Christian belief holds that angels were created in the time between the creation of the universe and the creation of human beings and that they have mind and spirit but no body. In C.E. 325, the Council of Nicea declared the belief in angels to be a valid dogma. The Catholic and Orthodox churches maintain that angels may be venerated but that they may not be worshipped. Catholic and Orthodox Christians pray to angels for intercession—much as they do saints. Both the Catholic and Orthodox churches teach that we are each given a guiding angel at the moment of conception.

In the Divine Liturgy, Eastern Orthodoxy's Eucharistic service, believers are brought into the presence of "thousands of archangels and hosts of angels, the Cherubim and Seraphim, six-winged, many-eyed, soaring aloft on their pinions, singing the triumphal hymn, shouting, crying out loud and saying, 'Holy! Holy! Holy!' "

Protestant belief says that although angels may exist, praying to them for intercession is unnecessary, and, for some Protestants, forbidden.

Jewish belief views angels as spiritual beings whose gift it is to serve God. Called "God's sons," angels are thought to make up "the court of God." The Talmud says that every child is assigned 11,000 angels at birth. There are almost this many descriptions of angels in rabbinical literature. Early rabbinical mystical tradition holds that the seven hallways leading to the vision of the Divine Throne (as described in Ezekiel) are guarded by angels.

Here is a favorite Catholic and Orthodox children's prayer.

THE GUARDIAN ANGEL PRAYER

Angel of God
My Guardian dear,
To whom God's love
Commits me here,
Ever this day
Be at my side
To light, to guard,
To rule and guide.
Amen.

Still, many Jewish scholars doubt the validity of angelology, and angels aren't even mentioned in the Mishnah. In the Passover text, it's made clear that Israel was delivered not by angelic intervention but by the help of God Himself.

Zoroastrianism is perhaps responsible for our perception of

THE BIBLE'S MOST FANTASTICAL DESCRIPTION OF HEAVENLY HOSTS APPEARS IN EZEKIEL 1:4–11 (KING JAMES VERSION)

I looked and, behold, a whirlwind came out of the north, a great cloud, and a fire enfolding itself, and a brightness was about it . . . and out of the mist thereof came the likeness of four living creatures. And this was their appearance: they had the likeness of a man. And every one had four faces, and every one had four wings. And their feet were straight feet; and the sole of their feet was like the sole of a calf's foot: and they sparkled like the color of burnished brass. And they had the hands of a man under their wings on their four sides . . . and their wings were joined one to another; they turned not when they went; they went every one straight forward. As for the likeness of their faces, they four had the face of a man, and the face of a lion on the right side: and they four had the face of an ox on the left side; they four also had the face of an eagle . . . and their wings were stretched upward; two wings of every one were joined one to another, and two cover their bodies.

Altogether, Ezekiel describes seven angels. The seven angels of Ezekiel may be compared with the seven eyes of Yahweh in Zechariah.

ANGELS' WORK

Angels, at least as seen from different religious perspectives, don't all use the wings-and-halo uniform. Instead, they all have essentially the same three-part job to do:

- Angels worship God and encourage people to do the same.
- They serve as heralds or liaisons between God and humankind.
- They act as caretakers for people— while remaining careful to never interfere with our free will.

Every army has its sergeants.

GREGORY THE GREAT'S SEVEN ARCHANGELS

- Michael
- Gabriel
- Raphael
- Uriel
- Simiel
- Orfiel
- Zachariel

ZOROASTRIANISM'S HOLY IMMORTALS: THE SEVEN *AMESHTA SPENTAS*

- Ahura Mazda (Spenta Mainyu): protector of humankind
- Vohu Manah: protector of cattle
- Asha: protector of fire
- Khshathra: protector of the heavens
- Haurvatat: protector of the waters
- Armaiti: protector of the Earth
- Ameretat: protector of plants and trees

angels and their work. Zoroastrians believe that angels have dominion over nations and that they work to bring each to a better understanding of good.

Moslems believe that although angels existed before the creation of people, humankind is seen by God as His greatest work, and therefore angels are required to bow down before people. Muhammad once had a vision in which the archangel Gabriel came to him and promised to guide his work as prophet. Moslems also believe that angels serve as witnesses on Judgment Day. Angels are also busy performing the duty of scribe whenever a Moslem is at prayer.

There are also angels breaking rocks in places other than heaven. According to the Bible's book of Revelation, a full one third of the angels joined in Lucifer's ill-advised rebellion and were sent to hell. In the fifteenth century, the bishop of Tusculum counted how many angels had fallen: 133,306,668, he said.

The celestial labor pool has been thoroughly classified by Eugene Marcher in his *Encyclopedia of Angels*. The popular perception of angelic beings did not begin with the Judeo-Christian formulation, however. From the earliest times, people who believed their gods were stars or planets or terrestrial objects also believed in spiritual beings who were often seen as benevolent mediators—but also sometimes as tormentors sent to punish or test people.

Naturally, where there are angels, there must also be saints.

SAINTLINESS

WHAT IT TAKES

The requirements of the only two churches still capable of calling a saint a saint—the Roman Catholic Church and the Orthodox Church—vary widely.

Roman Catholic Church

The Roman Catholic process of canonization is the final step in a long passage that begins with several well-timed miracles. To be considered for canonization, a candidate must first be beatified. While the candidate is in that state, at least two independently verifiable miracles must be ascribed to the candidate's intercession. Before beatification can take place, an inspection must have taken place, taken on by the local bishop. He examines both the life and work of the candidate as well as his or her general reputation for holiness. Miracles help, although martyrs are exempt from performing miracles to qualify for beatification—although a few are still necessary for full canonization. If the local inquiry seems to yield a legitimate result, Rome begins its own investigation—called the apostolic process—to determine whether the candidate was extraordinarily virtuous.

Beatification itself is an intermediary step to full saintliness; a blessed one may enjoy full saintly honors in a region or community. But only with full canonization can one ensure the universal veneration of the Roman Catholic church.

Orthodox Church

The Orthodox process is far less bureaucratic. An Orthodox saint may be simply an extraordinarily holy person, a great teacher, or someone beloved on an entirely local level—although very often, miracles are ascribed to those venerated as saints. The recent glorification of Saint John Maximovich of Shanghai and San Francisco has produced a spate of healings, interventions, and other miraculous occurrences.

Glorification of an Orthodox saint is a jurisdictional gesture. Those recognized as saints by the Russian church may not be recognized as saints by the Greek church, and vice versa. The result is a huge number of saints. The most recent comprehensive Orthodox calendar produced by Hieromonk Aidan Keller of the St. Hilarion

Monastery in Austin, Texas, lists some 12,000 saints. The Orthodox Church also recognizes all saints canonized by Rome before 1054, the year of the Great Schism between the Western and Eastern churches.

ALONG COMES MARY—AND OTHER APPARITIONS

The Apparition Litmus Test

Let's say you're taking a walk in the woods and you see a billowy white figure up ahead. Is it the neighbor chasing her dog? Or the Virgin Mary? Here's how the Roman Catholic Church tells for sure: First, the church gathers evidence. Authentic Marian apparitions (and the people who have discovered them) generally have had these elements in common:

- The one who witnessed the apparition usually shuns any publicity that accompanies the event.
- The witnesses are often quite young and apparently quite normal, although sometimes somewhat undereducated.
- The witnesses are rarely particularly devout before discovering the apparition.
- Apparitions are generally discovered in quiet and remote places.
- Apparitions are generally discovered in places or times of religious turmoil.
- Witnesses are often warned by Mary that the future will not be pleasant for them.
- Witnesses are able to give remarkably clear accounts of the apparition. Facts don't get blurry or distorted, and the witnesses usually don't contradict themselves while retelling the story.
- Witnesses are able to retell the story of the apparition for many years after the fact—again, without confusing the facts or contradicting earlier accounts.
- Witnesses receive a consistent message from the apparitions, invariably a call for increased prayer, repentance, and penance.
- Miraculous events usually occur during a sighting. Terminal illnesses may be cured without explanation, long-lost relatives may suddenly reappear, and so on.

When evaluating an apparition, the church classifies the sighting one of four ways:

- Initially, all sightings are considered to be *questionable*. Once the evidence is thoroughly examined and considered, a commission appointed by the local bishop will declare the sighting to be either false, fraudulent, or authentic.
- The apparition is *false* if the evidence doesn't support the assertion of the witness, even though the witness genuinely believes he or she saw the apparition and appears to be of sound mind.
- It's *fraudulent* if the evidence points toward a fabricated sighting for monetary gain, publicity, a need for attention, or other suspect reasons.
- It's classified as *authentic* only if the commission deemed it was unquestionably a supernatural event and the faith of others appeared to be strengthened by those who came in contact with the apparition.

Times and Places
The Virgin has appeared in various places at various times:

- *Rome.* Mary appears before Marisa Rossi at Via delle Benedettine 91, at least once a day, on every Sunday morning at 10:30, on the first Saturday of the month at 5:30 P.M., and on all Christian feast days. The ecclesiastical authority in Rome initiated a commission of inquiry in 1995, but an official statement has yet to be made.
- *Pescara, Italy.* Maria Fioritti saw Mary on a weekly basis in 1988. When 10,000 pilgrims arrived to share the vision, Mary didn't show.
- *Lubbock, Texas.* In 1988, on August 15 (the Feast of the Assumption), Mary made an appearance reported in the *New York Times:* "Then in the middle of mass, and shortly before dusk, the sun broke dramatically through a gathering curtain of clouds. Shrieks went up from the lawn, and many of the assembled cried, prayed and pointed toward the sky. Some said they saw Jesus in the heavens, some saw the Virgin Mary, some saw the gates of heaven." The *Times* also reported that others, including a number of priests, saw nothing unusual at all.
- *Marlboro, New Jersey.* From 1989 to 1992, Mary visited the home of Joseph Januszkiewicz on the same Sunday night of

each month. Eventually, thousands began flocking to the Januszkiewicz home.

- *Conyers, Georgia.* Beginning in October 1990, Nancy Fowler has been visited on the thirteenth of each month.
- *Denver.* Theresa Lopez was visited by Mary on the second Sunday of each month during 1992 at various locations around the city.
- *Cold Spring, Kentucky.* In the summer of 1992, Mary visited the Reverend Leroy Smith at St. Joseph's Catholic Church.

PREVIOUS MARIAN APPEARANCES	
DATE AND PLACE	WITNESSES
1531: Guadalupe, Mexico	Various; certified authentic by the Roman Catholic Church
1830: Paris	Catherine Laboure, a Sister of Charity; Catherine was subsequently canonized
1846: Salette, France	Two shepherds
1858: Lourdes	Fourteen-year-old Bernadette Soubirous
1871: Pontmain, France	
1879: Knock, Ireland	Margaret Beirne; the growing number of pilgrims to Knock inspired the construction of a huge international airport near the town
1917: Fatima, Portugal	Three shepherdesses, to whom Mary uttered a prophecy still kept secret by the surviving witnesses
1968–1971: Zeitoun, Egypt	Two Moslem auto mechanics
1981: Medjugorie of the former Yugoslavia	Daily updates through a woman named Maria Pavlovic

■ *Emmitsburg, Maryland.* Gianna Talone-Sullivan began seeing monthly apparitions of the Virgin in 1988.

Just outside El Nido, California (population 160), there's a billboard advertising a toll-free tele-apparition. The number on the sign is (800) 882-MARY.

Other apparitions of other sacred figures have also occurred. For instance, in 1823, Joseph Smith, founder of the Mormon Church (Church of Jesus Christ of Latter-Day Saints), was visited by an angel named Moroni, who gave Smith the new gospel, otherwise known as the Book of Mormon. In 1992, pilgrims to the "Jesus tree," a sycamore in a church parking lot in New Haven, Connecticut, saw the image of Christ between the branches. And in 1980, televangelist Oral Roberts had a vision of a 900-foot Jesus lifting his 60-story hospital up from the ground.

Veneration of the Virgin—called, by the Orthodox, the *theotókos,* or "God bearer"—is especially pronounced in Orthodox liturgical life, to a far greater degree than even in the Roman Catholic Church. However, Orthodoxy does not hold a belief in the Immaculate Conception of Mary because the Orthodox view of original sin does not

SAINTS WHO'LL NEVER MARCH FOR LOUIS ARMSTRONG

SAINT	PATRON SAINT OF	FEAST DAY
James the Great	those with rheumatoid arthritis	July 25
Gabriel	postal workers	September 29
Bernard	skiers	May 28
Ludwina	skaters	January 30
Anne	women in labor	February 24
Marin de Porres	beauticians	March 2
Vitus	comedians and jesters	May 12
Anthony of Padua	lost wanderers	June 25
Francis of Sales	the deaf	October 12
Genesius	government bureaucrats	August 16
Anthony Abbot	gravediggers	August 28
Amand	drunks	October 27
Britius	juvenile delinquents	February 12

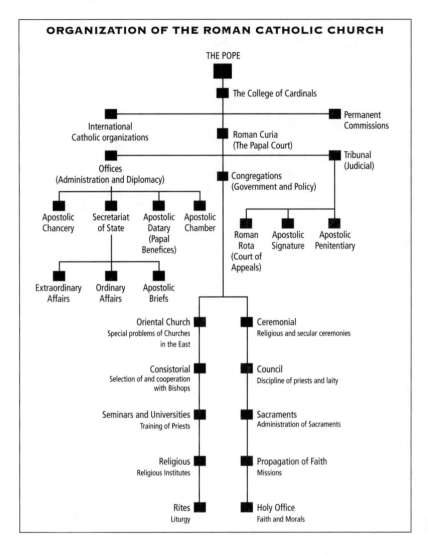

ORGANIZATION OF THE ROMAN CATHOLIC CHURCH

THE POPE

The College of Cardinals

Permanent Commissions

International Catholic organizations

Roman Curia (The Papal Court)

Tribunal (Judicial)

Offices (Administration and Diplomacy)

Congregations (Government and Policy)

Apostolic Chancery

Secretariat of State

Apostolic Datary (Papal Benefices)

Apostolic Chamber

Roman Rota (Court of Appeals)

Apostolic Signature

Apostolic Penitentiary

Extraordinary Affairs

Ordinary Affairs

Apostolic Briefs

Oriental Church — Special problems of Churches in the East

Ceremonial — Religious and secular ceremonies

Consistorial — Selection of and cooperation with Bishops

Council — Discipline of priests and laity

Seminars and Universities — Training of Priests

Sacraments — Administration of Sacraments

Religious — Religious Institutes

Propagation of Faith — Missions

Rites — Liturgy

Holy Office — Faith and Morals

agree with the Roman Catholic doctrine that all men and women are born in a state of sin. Rather, according to the Orthodox Church, men and women are born into a sinful world, of which mortality, the price of our fall from grace, is a part. So to the Orthodox, the Virgin is not seen as having been immaculately conceived, since, in Eastern theology, that would make her divine and not fully human. The Orthodox Church does claim, however, that her life was a sinless one.

For a full explanation of the differences between Roman Catholicism and Orthodoxy, see *Orthodox Dogmatic Theology: A Concise Exposition,* by Father Michael Pomazansky, and compare it to the recently revised catechism of the Roman Catholic Church.

Herbert Thurston and Donald Attwater's updating of *The Lives of the Saints* revived interest in Alban Butler's earlier work, and Attwater's *Saints of the East*—where we discover that the Coptic Church has a Saint Pontius Pilate—is also useful. More recently, not only is Sean Kelly and Rosemary Rogers's *Saints Preserve Us! Everything You Need to Know About Every Saint You'll Ever Need* a funny hagiography, but it's also quite accurate and more complete than most other *Lives.*

HERETICS!

There were heretics before Christianity. Some were garden-variety false prophets; some were temple priests gone bad. Perhaps the weirdest heretic was Egyptian Pharaoh Akhenaten, the only person in the whole history of heresy to be a heretic in the religion in which he was the god. But it was Christianity that turned the game of rooting out heretics into a major-league historical phenomenon.

Why? Because before Christianity, heresy lacked what media people today call global impact: The development of the church for the first three or four centuries of its existence followed the bureaucratic and political infrastructure of the Roman Empire. The church and the emperor worked hand in hand. Once established as a state religion by the Roman Empire in the fourth century, the church became the only politically acceptable religious institution in the Eastern world. The emperors were happy: They were now seen as earthly delegates of God's power—a status they hadn't enjoyed convincingly since the day mad Caligula declared himself divine. This relationship also served the interests of the church: With the force of the state hiding behind the altar screen, heresy became treason. That was because an alternative view on something dogmatically critical could threaten the stability of the governing system.

That didn't stop heresy, of course. It just raised the stakes. The real reason there was so much heresy in Christianity as an ethical system, as an explanation for creation, as a faith, is that the religion invited introspection. And that's an invitation to trouble.

	HERESIES:
CONCEPT	DESCRIPTION
Gnosticism (c. 140–250)	The sense that the spiritual world was good and the material world wasn't good led ultimately to the belief in two competing creators—the evil demiurge and its rival, good God. Gnostics believed that God was hidden by the fog of the material world and that salvation could be attained only through knowledge. Believers felt this vital insight could be attained through prayer and investigation. There were hundreds of differing Gnostic traditions. Many congregations were quite staid and in close harmony with the church. Others were more adventurous: Some, for instance, practiced communal marriages, and not a few were primitive communistic congregations. Almost all of them shied away from mystic, intuitive traditions. *Gnosis,* in Greek, means "knowledge."
	Gnosticism has been revived of late by esoteric New Age believers, some of whom are attracted to the notion of a more romantic Jesus figure. One recent book—*Holy Blood, Holy Grail*—follows Jesus through a mock crucifixion, then takes him and his lover, Mary Magdalen, on a cruise to the south of France, where the authors say Christ settled and started the Merovingian dynasty of French kings. The book contains a picture of a befuddled descendent of Jesus, a pharmacist, as it happens. The Naj'Hammādī texts are of mostly Gnostic origin.
Docetism (c. 150–present)	Docetists denied the reality of the human form and nature of Jesus, as the Son of God. They had no single explanation of Christ. Docetic theory found it difficult, if not impossible, to unite the Son of God with a human being, subjected to suffering and death. Some denied the fleshly birth, life, and death of Jesus Christ and claimed that His sufferings

A GUIDE TO UNWELCOME IDEAS

HERETIC	EFFECT
Valentinus, Carpocrates, the Naassenes	Surprisingly, the Gnostics were not driven out of the church. In fact, many never belonged in the first place, and there is one school of thought that holds that Gnosticism predated Christianity—not a far-fetched notion in view of its strong Zoroastrian flavor. Gnosticism was finally consumed by the growing social and political pervasiveness of the established church. Ironically, the Gnostic contemplative tradition did much to inform Christian mysticism. For a head-to-toe treatment, see Kurt Wilson and Robert Wilson's *Gnosis: The Nature and History of Gnosticism*.
Valentinus and the Gnostics	In the third century, Christological debates attempted to clarify the belief that Jesus Christ was truly a mortal, fleshly man. By the middle of the fourth century, Docetism was referred to by Theodoret as the complete denial of the humanity of Jesus. Through time, Docetism understood Jesus as a divine being.

CONCEPT	DESCRIPTION
Docetism (cont.)	were not real; others imagined Christ as a polymorphous divine being, appearing in different forms according to a person's ability to perceive Him. In the middle of the second century, many Gnostics thought that the spiritual reality of Christ represented the inner, spiritual part of Himself.
Montanism (c. 156–350)	The early growth of Christianity quickly outstripped the administrative ability of the church to monitor the doctrine of its members. To remedy this, the church took its first step toward secularization, adopting whatever apparatus of the state necessary to instruct and regulate its various congregations, who, up until this time, had simply been scattered groups of believers. This move inaugurated the church's grand-scale world mission. In 156, Montanus appeared and urged his followers to live a strict Christian life of asceticism and spirituality and to prepare for the apocalypse. Religious communities were formed for this purpose and large congregations were infiltrated with Montanists.
Arianism (c. 250–350)	The earliest heresies revolved around the concept of Christ's divinity. Paul's teaching, which advanced the case for a divine Christ, caused some of the biggest problems: Are there two gods, God and Jesus? If Jesus is the Son of God, then God came first, yes? But if God came first, then Jesus is not eternal, and how can a god be less than eternal?

HERETIC	EFFECT
	The term *Docetist* appears first in *History of the Church,* by Eusebius, in reference to those who spread the gospel of Peter, written in the middle of the second century. Clement of Alexandria attributed the term to Julius Cassianus, who most probably wrote the Naj'Hammādī treatise *Testimony of Truth.* Hippolytus referred to Docetism as a heresy based on a rationalist point of view concerning Christ. For further reading, see *The Christian Tradition,* Volume 1: *The Emergence of the Catholic Tradition,* by Jaroslav Pelikan.
Montanus and, later, two female converts—Maximilla and Prisca.	The movement finally expired because of a lack of divinely inspired enthusiasm for religious strictness. Its expiration, along with the successful suppression of Gnosticism (see above), effectively created the Catholic Church. Eusebius's commentaries contain an interesting account of the growth of Montanism. But the movement's most influential backer was Tertullian, some of whose works survive.
Arius	Athanasius won, Jesus was declared to be of the same substance of God, Arius went into exile, and heresy became political. See John Norman Davidson Kelly's *Early Christian Doctrines* for more information.

CONCEPT	DESCRIPTION
Arianism (cont.)	One unfortunate answer was provided by Arius (250–336), a bishop of Alexandria. The Arian heresy said that Jesus was indeed divine, but, since He was created by God, He was not one with the substance with God. Arius's rival, Athanasius (296–373), later named bishop of Alexandria, responded by saying that Jesus and God were co-eternal and co-equal. Emperor Constantine—who made Christianity the Roman Empire's state religion after having a dream of the Cross before the Battle of Milvian Bridge in 312, which secured his imperial ambition—called the Council of Nicaea in 325 to decide this burning question.
Pelagianism (sixth century)	Pelagianism was a British heresy that argued with Augustine's view that only divine grace can cause salvation and that some people were predestined to damnation. Pelagians argued that people have free will and can help save themselves by exercising their righteousness.
Apollinarianism (fourth century)	Apollinarians believed that the divine *Logos*, or Word, took the place of the rational soul in Jesus.
Nestorianism (fifth century)	Nestorians felt the title *theotókos,* or "God bearer," was not appropriate for the Virgin Mary, because she bore the human nature of Jesus and not His divine nature.
Priscillianism (c. 375–450)	Priscillianism denied that Christ existed before He was born.
Albigensianism (c. 1200)	The Albigenses in southern France rejected the physical world as inherently evil. The Albigensian theory was that God created

HERETIC	EFFECT
Pelagius, a troublesome monk	Pelagius was condemned as a heretic for his trouble. But the force behind Pelagianism was irresistible and ultimately came to influence later church reformers.
Apollinaris the Younger, bishop of Laodicea in Syria	Condemned by the Council of Constantinople in 381.
Nestorius, archbishop of Constantinople	Condemned at the Council of Ephesus in 431 and exiled to upper Egypt—where a Nestorian church soon flourished.
Priscillian, bishop of Ávila	Priscillian was executed in 386, the first to be done in for heresy, but not the last.
	The pope, Innocent III, tried to convert the Albigenses. When that failed, he launched a crusade, under Simon de

CONCEPT	DESCRIPTION
Albigensianism (cont.)	spirit; evil created matter. The spirits were held in the matter, transmigrating from one body to another until they paid for their various naughtinesses and went to heaven, thereby liberating their souls from hideous flesh. To the Albigenses, Christ was really an angel in a phantom body, and the church had corrupted His true meaning. Rejecting the sacraments and advocating extreme asceticism, the Albigenses delayed baptism until the moment before death.
Catharianism (c. 1200)	Closely aligned to Albigensianism was the Cathar movement. Cathars were zealous dualists. Their firm belief in the inherent evil of the material world made them forswear all physical pleasures, including sex. In their dietary laws, they were strict vegans (although fish was allowed). Their popular appeal was based on an almost universal admiration for their faith in the face of violent persecution.
Waldensianism (c. 1182–1550)	The Waldensians practiced unauthorized preaching, using vernacular translations from the Bible. They adhered to a literal interpretation of Christ's gospel teachings, and therefore believed that God's laws came before human laws.
	Waldensians believed they were the church to whom apostolic succession had passed, rather than to the church as led by the pope. To them, Roman priests were not true priests. They thought that any man or woman, if pure in mind and acts, could function as a God-ordained priest. Waldensians rejected the Roman Catholic Church's sacraments and most of its ceremonies and prayers. They did

HERETIC	EFFECT
	Montfort, to correct their errors. In 1209, de Montfort rode into Béziers and killed about 20,000 people. Subsequently, in 1233, Pope Gregory IX decided to eliminate all heretics and authorized the establishment of tribunals of inquiry to discover and punish the unorthodox. (See Inquisitions, page 114.)
	The best source of information on this astonishing event is Walter L. Wakefield and Austin P. Evans's *Heresies of the High Middle Ages*.
	The movement died out in the fifteenth century.
	For a survey of both Albigensianism and Catharism, see Walter L. Wakefield and Austin P. Evans's *Heresies of the High Middle Ages* and Joseph R. Strayer's *The Albigensian Crusades*.
Pierre Valdes, Lyons, France	In 1182, Valdes and his followers were excommunicated.
	In 1184, at the Council of Verona, the Waldensians were among the heretical groups condemned by the church of Rome. Of all the sects condemned, the Waldensians were the only group not to have been absorbed by another religious order or to disappear as a sect.
	Valdes died in approximately 1210, but in 1205 a schism developed between the Lombard Waldenists and the northern Waldenists. The Lombards organized their own sacraments, settled in towns, and elected their own leaders. The northern

CONCEPT	DESCRIPTION
Waldensianism (cont.)	practice, however, their own forms of baptism, marriage, and confession. They also rejected all nonspiritual activities, such as mandating legal authority and waging war. Taking a vow of poverty, they wandered throughout southeastern France, into northern Italy, and even into Germany, gaining the support mainly of artisans and peasants and living off the generosity of their converts.
Hussitism (c. 1400–1600)	The Hussites represented a Bohemian church reform movement based loosely on the predestinarian teachings of John Wycliffe's Lollard movement. Like the Waldensians, the Hussites were repulsed by the excesses and impiousness of the Roman Catholic clergy and by the rapacious appetites of the church administration. By appealing to nationalistic sentiment and democratic reform of agriculture, the Hussites quickly grew in importance.

HERETIC	EFFECT
	Waldenists, following Valdes, retained their practices of poverty and wanderings and firmly believed that Christ was the one and only leader. In the fourteenth century, the Waldenists had become a mainly northern phenomenon, with strongholds in Germany and central Europe, and continued preaching as Christ's apostles, secretly visiting their believers and administering their versions of the sacraments. They survived to become one of the reformed churches of the sixteenth century, with their own congregations and religious forms. Their popularity rested on the fact that they preached without metaphysical and theological implications and that they remained closest to the teachings of the gospel. Their influence can be seen on the Hussites. For more on this influential movement, see Malcolm D. Lambert's *Medieval Heresy: Popular Movements from Bogomil to Hussites.*
John Huss (1373–1415)	Despite launching crusades, persecutions, and, at least once, all-out war against the Hussites, Rome was unable to suppress the Hussite movement. The Hussite tradition was ultimately absorbed by the Protestant Reformation.

A DOZEN REASONS WHY PROTESTANTS PROTESTED

After 1,500 years as the sole voice of Christianity in the West, the Roman Catholic Church had reached a fairly advanced state of good old-fashioned secular decadence, especially in its parochial life. In 1517, an Augustinian priest, Martin Luther, challenged his Dominican nemesis, Johann Tetzel, to a debate on 95 points of disagreement. Luther issued his invitation to debate by tacking his list of talking points to the church door in Wittenberg. The result was a century and a half of Catholic disintegration.

Catholic historians, blessed with hindsight, calculate 12 reasons why the Western church splintered:

1. *Unresponsive authority:* The growing power of the Roman Curia and its subordinate bureaucracy was resented by everybody who came into even indirect contact with it.
2. *Weakened basis for authority:* Four popes resided in Avignon—and they were followed by two more antipopes. The politicalization of the papacy by the French court did little to strengthen the authority of the church. And neither did the rather hideous excesses, worldliness, and debauchery of several of the occupants of Peter's throne.
3. *Local politics:* Many of the bishops who questioned papal authority were in actuality temporal, not ecclesiastical, princes. It was in their interests to undermine the authority of Rome and advance their own.
4. *Poorly chosen priests:* Many of the men in clerical orders were unfit—spiritually, academically, temperamentally—for their jobs.
5. *Monastic power:* Many of the church's institutions—notably, the great monasteries—had, by 1500, amassed great wealth and power. At the same time, these institutions gave little to the surrounding communities and were preoccupied with their own internal political wars.
6. *Indifference:* Many Christians just didn't care who won the struggle for the church's purse strings and power.
7. *Governmental ambition:* Lutheranism was almost instantly made a state church in Saxony, giving the elector a useful

tool with which to leverage money and power from Catholic institutions. The same thing happened almost overnight throughout northern Europe.

8. *Breakdown of the old order:* Feudalism was in full collapse by 1500, and the resulting social disorder made a Protestant church an almost natural consequence of a protestant society.

9. *Humanism:* The rise of humanistic thought and the so-called Renaissance made the monolithic intellectual power of the church philosophically untenable.

10. *Animism:* At the same time, social unrest among the lowest classes stimulated the growth of neo pagan quasi-religions.

11. *Materialism:* The global economy, stimulated by the end of feudalism and the new emphasis on exploration and science, stirred a kind of general societal restlessness. The world grew dissatisfied with the sedentary nature of the church.

12. *Publicity:* The new technology used by the printing press was quickly adopted by those who wished to spread propaganda against the church.

Obviously, the Catholic Church was in need of reform, or the Reformation would never have been so completely successful or so quickly embraced. But the Reformation—and the apparently consequent Counter-Reformation—were not specific events. Rather, they were manifestations of the social pressures under which the church was operating in Europe. In some parts of Europe—notably, the German states and England—dismantling the instruments of power and seizing the valuable property of the Roman church was a desirable thing to do from a political point of view.

For a wonderfully readable survey of the Reformation, look into Hilaire Belloc's *How the Reformation Happened.* Paul Johnson's *History of Christianity* also covers this turf well. There was never a reformation in the Eastern Church. There were many reform-minded patriarchs, though. See Sir Steven Runciman's *Great Church in Captivity: A Study of Patriarchate of Constantinople from the Eve of the Turkish Conquest to the Greek War of Independence.*

In other parts of Europe—notably Spain and France—maintaining the power of the Roman church was essential. In Spain, especially, the reaction against the disintegration of ecclesiastical authority elsewhere was dramatically severe. The Inquisition, for example, was a Spanish invention, used first against Moors and Jews, but then against heretics, especially Calvinists.

INQUISITIONS

Near the end of the twentieth century, we learned how thrilling life can be when those who claim to possess the moral edge have an army to help them enforce their authority. An armed bureaucracy has shown we have the ability to make little Wacos everywhere—remember the standoff there in 1993 between law-enforcement officers and a religious group called the Branch Davidians?—not only in Waco, Texas, itself but anywhere an individual or a group seeks to do anything mainstream Americans might see as a little odd. It no longer requires much imagination to conjure the image of a knock on the door from the People's Police for the American Way or to consider the interesting maneuvers of a Militant Environmentalist Majority.

The reason this all seems even somewhat plausible is that every now and then these sorts of odd things actually come to pass, and the result inevitably is a demonstration of the terrible overbite you get when you give political correctness real teeth. Take the Inquisition, for instance. Sure, it was a bit excessive, but it certainly diminished the noise of unpopular debate. Here's the way it worked:

- The inquisitors came into a town, perhaps like Béziers, and asked that everyone who had sinned, heresywise, come forward and confess.
- Those who did come forward were given easy punishments—maybe a spell of fasting or a pilgrimage to complete.
- Then, after the inquisitors had allowed a month or so for sinners to come forward, the pace quickened. The parish priest would summon all his congregants to come before the inquisitor and a group of clergy and laity.
- If at least two people accused someone of something—*any-thing*—the inquisitor held a summary hearing, rather like the child-abuse and sexual-harassment witch-hunts of the 1990s.

The inquiring minds of the Inquisition wanted to know exactly how guilty the accused was.

▪ If the accused didn't confess, he or she was thrown into prison.

Around 1252, after nearly two decades of social and ecclesiastical housecleaning, a major advance in speeding up the inquisitorial process was made. Pope Innocent IV decided to allow torture as a means of making the jobs of those seeking confessions a little easier.

If, by chance, the accused was condemned to death—as opposed to expiring midtorture—the church would not carry out the sentence, leaving such executions to the civil authorities.

Earlier, in 1320, Pope John XXII had told the inquisitors to deal with witches as well as heretics. This new demographic segment added about 30,000 more deaths over the ensuing 150 years. A very scary book, not available in all libraries, is the *Malleus Maleficarum* (*The Hammer of Witchcraft*), written by two Dominican witch-hunters; it describes in detail how to deal with witches, "of which the world is being over run."

CROSSES TO BEAR

We've all got them. In fact, crosses—as elements of ornamentation as well as symbols of belief—are all over history. Cave people even drew them; only the circle is more ubiquitous as a well-loaded graphic statement.

> **TORQUEMADA AND THE SPANISH INQUISITION**
>
> The Spanish Inquisition, which began during the reign of Columbus's patrons, King Ferdinand and Queen Isabella, is generally accepted as the mother of all inquisitions. It ran for several hundred years; the last burning at the stake was in Seville in 1781. The first grand inquisitor was the famous monk Tomás de Torquemada. He is credited with about 2,000 toastings, the preferred method of heretic disposal. *The Spanish Inquisition,* by Henry Kamen, is a disquieting, but not torturous, study.

As an instrument of law enforcement, however, crosses have a more trackable history. Punishment by crucifixion was used by everybody in antiquity, including Assyria, Egypt, Persia, Greece, Carthage, Macedonia, and (most famously) by Rome. The Egyptian "cross" is a shortchanged version, barely describing a T. The Etrusco-Indo-Sino–Native Americo *svastika* (Sanskrit), a symbol passed around the human species like an old sock, needed Nazis to make it truly infamous.

There are two ways a person was killed by crucifixion. One way was the way the Romans killed Christ: scourging and beating, then nailing or binding the person to a cross and leaving him or her to die. The other way was, if possible, even worse: Bound to a stake, the prisoner was stripped, partially skinned, partially eviscerated, then, if possible, made to carry the stake to the place of execution, where he or she was either bound to it or impaled on it. Either way, death by crucifixion was understood to be horrific. Christ's triumph over the cross gave the symbol a terrifically powerful significance, which it shared with other symbols, including the fish.

Not until the reign of Constantine, however, did the cross assume the public status of religious logo. Once established as the universal symbol of Christianity, the cross quickly developed a wide variety of applications, some informed by an association with a famous saint—such as the cross of Saint Andrew, depicting an X-shaped device on which the first-called disciple was supposed to have been killed—and some informed by traditional depictions, such as the three-bar Orthodox cross, with its top bar representing the inscription that was alleged to have been attached to the top of Christ's cross, mocking him as "king of the Jews," and its lower bar representing the footplate upon which Christ's feet were attached, with the right side tilted up to signify the good thief executed next to Jesus.

MEDIEVALISM AND THE EASTERN CHURCH

The Byzantine Empire, the remnant of Rome's global operation, lasted until late in the afternoon of May 29, 1453, and, despite the empire's many vicissitudes, imperial subjects never suffered a Dark Ages. Instead, they suffered land grabs by Arab invaders, pillaging by Roman Catholic crusaders, and eventual conquest by Turkish Moslems. So instead of a reformation, the Eastern Orthodox Church suffered other punishments inflicted more casually by history: The thousand-year occupation of Orthodox lands and the forced conversion of Orthodox Christians by Moslems, for instance, has been followed by a Soviet regime that killed millions of Orthodox clerics and faithful.

In recent years, the Orthodox, having successfully avoided creating their own homegrown Protestants, now face Western Protestant missionaries flocking to Russia hoping to carve out some

> Sir Steven Runciman's *Fall of Constantinople* is an accurate, highly readable account of the last days of the world's greatest empire.

territory before the Russian Orthodox Church has a chance to recover from its long ordeal. For many years, the Orthodox saw Protestants as a problem peculiar to the Roman Catholic Church. No more.

Today, Orthodox churches are divided into patriarchates, which generally correspond to national borders. The Romanian Orthodox Church has its own patriarch, for example, as do the Orthodox churches of Russia, Finland, Bulgaria, and other Orthodox countries. Countries in which Orthodoxy is a relatively late arrival—such as the United States or Australia—and countries in which Soviet domination, once removed, has led to the emergence of national churches to rival the Russian Orthodox church—such as in the Ukraine—suffer under uncanonical circumstances in which several jurisdictions compete for worshippers. All Orthodox churches, however, are bound together by Orthodox theology, and there is no significant disagreement about what an Orthodox Christian should believe.

MONASTICISM

It took almost four centuries before zealous Christian desert hermits finally organized small communities to allow for communal prayer and a little mutual support. These simple goals remain the main concern of monastics, but the various rules under which a monk lives will have a great deal of impact on how he achieves those goals.

In Roman Catholicism, the Rule of Saint Benedict has shaped the Western monastic experience. The multitude of orders of friars—preaching monks—and other orders, such as the Jesuits, have made Catholic monasticism a dynamic part of the church's mission. The influence of monasticism on the church during the medieval period, when monks saved a great deal of classical culture, can't be underestimated.

Orthodox monasticism has no separate orders; all monks (and nuns) belong to a single category of religious contemplative, devoted to prayer, self-discipline, and achievement of a kind of mystical inner peace (hesychasm). Most monks live communally, but several clusters of sketes—loose confederations of hermits—also exist. The semi-autonomous "republic" of Mount Áthos, on a peninsula near Thessalonica, is governed by monks from the various monasteries on the holy mountain. Women are forbidden entry. This mysterious place is the principal source of Orthodox monastic activity, as well as a valuable resource of monastic influence.

Orthodox monks come in three varieties:

- Rasophores live the life of the monastery but take no vows.
- Monks of "greater" and "lesser" habits take vows of permanent chastity, obedience, and commitment.
- Starets are monks who have demonstrated profound holiness and spiritual wisdom. They act as spiritual guides for others.

NEW AGE MYSTICISM

The slide toward cultural secularism that began in the sixteenth century has contrived to make traditional religions appear inconsequential by removing from them (often with great willingness from various denominations) their most valuable role—that of providing the framework not for a system of belief but for a way of life. Today, for many people religion is just too much trouble, too politically incorrect, or just too embarrassing to pursue with total conviction.

As a result, many people, experiencing spiritual malnourishment, have sought other more socially acceptable forms of religious expression. Many of these have antecedents in antiquity—such as the Gaia cult—whereas others are brand spanking new. Many are hybrid expressions of Oriental religious customs commingled with Western psychology, a focus on health, and sometimes politics as a necessary adjunct. Few people actually claim "New Age" as their religion, yet the University of California estimates that there are 12 million or more Americans who are somehow active in the New Age movement and another 30 million who are "avidly interested." If you put those two groups together, you would have the third largest religion in the United States. Meanwhile, *American Demographics* magazine recently studied the readership of another magazine, *New Age Journal,* and came up with some surprising statistics: The circulation of the journal increased by a factor of nine during the 1980s. Some 90 percent of the magazine's readers are college grads and are three times more likely to take part in civic activities than the average person. In marketing terms, this is an attractive demographic indeed.

That hasn't escaped the attention of those with something to sell:

- Author and surgeon Bernie S. Siegel, whose books—with titles like *Love, Medicine, & Miracles* and *Peace, Love, and Healing*—have sold millions of copies.
- Actress Shirley MacLaine, whose books *Out on a Limb* and *Dancing in the Light* have brought psychics, channelers, healers, and guides into the homes of millions.
- M. Scott Peck, a psychiatrist whose book *The Road Less Traveled* is the longest running best-seller in American publishing history.
- Deepak Chopra, doctor and author of books with titles like *Ageless Body, Timeless Mind: The Quantum Alternative to Growing Old.*

It would be unfair to suggest that these people are cynically exploiting the culture's spiritual poverty. At first, New Age ideas seemed goofy to the general populace—but then, they slowly crept into the minds and vocabulary of the masses. For instance, creative visualization—considered a silly hippie thing in the 1960s and 1970s—became big business in the 1990s. Pro sports teams, major corporations, and others pay big bucks to consultants (many of whom are ex-hippies) to master the art of creative visualization, because it is now a proven technique for success. Cancer patients are taught to imagine themselves well, and it sometimes works.

It's helpful to examine the New Age movement in the context of other, more easily understood religious movements. For example, in many important ways, the New Age clerics are strict sectarians, creating doctrine and dogma as they go and succeeding or failing on how well others find they are doing in their jobs.

In fact, despite the notion that New Age beliefs generally spring from a liberal view of things, the new religious movements actually have a lot in common with very traditional religious beliefs, such as those found in conservative Christianity:

- "Right" living
- A personal connection to God
- Spiritual renewal, or the experience of being "born again"

The very familiarity we all have by now with organized, mainstream religion seems to mitigate against its ultimate success. But the truth is somewhat different: We know no more—and, in some important ways, less—about God and our relationship with God's creation now than ever. New research is demonstrating the power of prayer to heal the sick. Health surveys are showing that people involved in old-fashioned religions live longer, happier lives than naysayers and agnostics. Marriages last longer, children grow up healthier, lives are generally enriched by conventional religious experiences and expression. Must be something in the water.

Index